The Ten Rules of High Performance Living

Barnet Meltzer, M.D.

Foreword by Carl Lewis

Sourcebooks, Inc.
Naperville, IL

Publisher's Note

It is our intention that the information in this book be used solely under the guidance and supervision of a qualified health professional. Diligent efforts have been made to assure the accuracy and safety of this information for a general audience. Nonetheless, different individuals require different health care needs. This book is not intended to provide medical advice, nor is it to be used as a substitute for advice from your own physician. The information is presented without guarantees from the author and publisher, who disclaim all liability or responsibility in connection with any mishaps or damage caused, or alleged to be caused, directly or indirectly, by the information contained in this book.

Published by Sourcebooks, Inc.
P.O. Box 372, Naperville, Illinois 60566
(630) 961-3900
FAX: (630) 961-2168

Library of Congress Cataloging-in-Publication Data
Meltzer, Barnet.
    The ten rules of high performance living/Barnet Meltzer; foreword by Carl Lewis.
        p.   cm.
    ISBN 1-57071-208-5
    1. Health. 2. Mental health. 3. Success.   I. Title.
RA776.9.M44   1998
613—dc21   97-51867
                                                                        CIP

Printed and Bound in the United States of America
10   9   8   7   6   5   4   3   2   1

TO TRUTH-SEEKING SOULS who still hold dear the American dream. Health, happiness, and success built into a balanced lifestyle will be the emerging issue of the twenty-first century. This book is the dream-catcher to give you the tools to achieve your dream. Its purpose is to help you find value amidst a challenging, stressful, and confusing era. The focus is on high performance, unbridled fulfillment.

Contents

Foreword

THERE ARE MANY interesting challenges in life, not the least of which is to stay well and fit throughout your life. *The Ten Rules of High Performance Living* can make the difference between a life of vitality and wellness or one of disease. Dr. Meltzer is a well-respected, internationally known, Board Certified physician. He is recognized for his integrative approach to balancing the mind, the body, the heart, and the soul. These ten rules will empower you with a step-by-step formula to develop the strategies, technique, and skills to strengthen your body, enrich your immune system, and enhance the quality of your life. It teaches you how to become a champion in your own life. It has helped me and thousands of others!

Carl Lewis,
Olympic Gold Medalist,
1984, 1988, 1992, 1996

Acknowledgments

THE AUTHOR GRATEFULLY acknowledges the support of loved ones, friends, and patients who are in great measure responsible for this book. Special thanks to Michelle LoBue, Richard Levak, and Karen Bouris for believing in me. Without their inspiration, this book would not have been born. Thank you to Todd Stocke for all your help.

Introduction

THERE IS ONLY one way to start this introduction, and that is to tell you what is on my mind. I strongly believe the best way to fully enjoy your life and achieve lasting fulfillment is to be totally healthy and fit in mind, body, heart, and soul. Life is a most precious gift.

As we approach the juncture of the new millennium, we are arriving at a decisive moment of truth. We are drifting away from the great American dream of achieving success without sacrificing health and happiness. The pursuit of wealth, power, technological efficiency, prosperity, financial security, and corporate or personal achievement has created so much stress that the great majority of Americans over age thirty-five are struggling. They are either experiencing burnout, overload, confusion in their primary love relationships, or going through breakdowns in their family life

I love life and being alive. By no means am I an alarmist— I care. I have supervised over thirty thousand patients in my practice and have been gifted with vision in the arena of human affairs. I see an impending crisis in the United States. The biggest danger lies in the fact that the country's leadership and much of its media are burying their heads in the sand. The truth is that emotional stress, emotional dysfunction, emotional deprivation, and emotional entanglement are becoming a way of life on this planet. Too many people feel trapped. In fact, toxic inflationary stress levels, commercialized lifestyles, nutritional self-abuse, high-density environmental pollution, addictive behavior, dysfunctional relationships, and dysfunctional parenting have suddenly become the major impediment to sustaining healthy, happy, fulfilling high performance lifestyles.

Someone has to take the wheel. We need to define success in the context of a balanced life of happiness, fulfillment, and wellness at home, at work, or at play. Unless you take charge of your life, artificial lifestyles, toxic stress, and fear-oriented belief systems will give a balanced reality a run for its money.

Yes, I am referring to the quality of your life. We all have a unique purpose, and only those who experience high level, high performance mental, emotional, spiritual, and physical wellness can take their cause or message to its fullest potential. I have written this book to motivate and hopefully inspire you to live out your dream.

High Performance Living will teach you how to stay vital, fit, enthusiastic, and potent. Your physical condition and attitude have everything to do with High Performance Living, and a High Performance Lifestyle enables you to sustain your dream.

The key is that High Performance Living prevents disease. High Performance Living is far superior to curing any illness. Hopefully, you won't have to learn the hard way that the least costly illness is the one that never occurs. Why is it that for so many it seems that a crisis is the only way to let go of your past and face up to what you are and what the essence of your life is about? If you are unsure of what I mean, just ask a parent, relative, or friend what a stroke, coronary disease, arthritis, kidney failure, hip replacements, or cancer have done to their ability to stay active mentally or physically.

Maybe you think it won't happen to you. Don't kid yourself! It can happen to anyone who doesn't have a foolproof high performance health plan in the same way you can run out of money without wisely planned finances.

Every day, hundreds of physicians send thousands of patients to their local pharmacies to purchase drugs. Yet, there is one prescription you can't buy over the counter...high fitness and High Performance Living in mind, body, heart, and soul are not for sale. They cannot be packaged, shelved, or preserved. So what can you do? There is an alternative to the stressful, undesirable lifestyle of burnout, fatigue, anger, obesity, and breakdown. I call it the Ten Rules of High Performance Living. Here is how it works:

One day in the back chambers of my office in Del Mar, California, I came to a shocking, yet simple realization:

Abundant, vital, rejuvenating, natural life energies
lie dormant within.

Medical science calls it the "immune system." The immune system has the magnificent potential to empower all of us to achieve High Performance Living. In other words, your immune system is a self-renewing, self-repairing, natural pharmacy. When it operates well, it energizes and inspires you to be the best at who you are. I find it interesting that emotional stress, addictive, self-destructive habits, negative thinking, nutritional abuse, depression, and self-abusive behavior degenerate and destroy your immune system. Are you going to allow immune dysfunction to take all the fun out of your life?

The Ten Rules of High Performance Living is a proven wellness formula to simplify, lighten up, and balance your life. In the same way that your computer or VCR came with an operating manual, this operating manual gives you the tools, know-how, and strategies to help you design your individualized high performance lifestyle.

With this take-charge program, you can look forward to:

- penetrating personal fulfillment
- sustained vitality
- peak physical performance
- superior personal achievement
- enduring productivity

The long-lasting benefits of this wellness plan come from following its specific techniques. Its formula empowers you to:

- sustain endless energy
- zap burnout
- prevent accelerated aging
- strengthen your willpower
- keep sexually active
- lighten-up your state of mind
- heighten your self-worth
- inspire vital enthusiasm

How you structure, stick to, and design your own formula has everything to do with living your dream life.

This book will guide you to realize your highest potential for health, sustained vitality, self-expression, productivity, unconditional love, fitness, fulfillment, and meaningful service in your life. The ten-point formula is simple and well-organized to create a tough and practical order that is on the horizon; you will need a keen sense of balance, willpower, faith, love, and inner-strength.

Determination, consistency, and courage become everything when it comes to living your truth.

Just as government is no government without self-responsibility, managed care is no health care without self-care and self-discipline.

In the final analysis, the quality of your life is the story behind the kind of nourishment you get. When you are totally thriving and experiencing the benefits of a high performance lifestyle, it is no accident. You are living, loving, eating, and thinking correctly. This ten-point formula is timeless, because it gives you pearls for achieving a balance between health, happiness, and success that come from places ranging from the Orient to the Andes. Whether you live a high performance lifestyle or suffer from frustrating, chronic dissatisfaction, it is your choice.

We are all at a crucial, decisive stage in determining our future prospects for lasting health and happiness. I believe this book can be the turning point in your life. It will hold true to its reputation for being a dream-catcher and will help you realize your dreams. My point is simple. Without great health, you cannot sustain high performance relationships with your spouse, your kids, your co-workers, or yourself.

Balance is the foundation for vital, healthy living. As you embrace its principles and positive living habits, your families will thrive as will your children, your friends, and your career. After all, we all have dreams to be fulfilled, and without our dreams, our passion for life breaks down. But, we need a new approach to create this balance. This book is the first practical, simple-to-follow, true-to-life manual that gives you the tools to create High Performance Living. Only those well-nourished souls experiencing the balance of high-level emotional, spiritual, mental, and physical wellness will be capable of effectively meeting the incredible challenges of the new millennium. Get involved, stay committed, and accept full responsibility for your life. Above all, take things in stride, stay light-hearted, and fully appreciate your journey on the road to High Performance Living.

How to Use This Book

CONGRATULATIONS! By purchasing *The Ten Rules of High Performance Living*, you have just taken the first step into a whole new world of greater health, happiness, and success. To reach your goals, you will need to apply the ten rules to your life on a consistent basis.

To obtain the best results from this program, I suggest that you read the whole book first before engaging the interactive self-assessments present in each chapter. Then, after completing the written text, focus on one rule at a time. After completing the interactive section in Rule #1, "Simplify Your Life," for instance, apply the information to your daily life. When you are comfortable with your progress, take up the second rule. Follow the chapters in sequence. In this manner, each subsequent rule builds on the one before. Do not rush to complete this book, and bear in mind that High Performance Living may require some fundamental changes in your lifestyle or thinking. Allow yourself time for self-analysis and soul searching. Give yourself time to incorporate the ten-point formula into your life.

Be easy on yourself. Your goal is to make permanent changes, so take it easy and, above all, be proud of your effort. Believe in love, and believe in yourself.

Once you have completed the entire text, I recommend that you get back to basics every three months, at the time of your seasonal cleansing. At that time, review your progress, and score yourself from one to ten on each rule, with ten being the best. Then, determine what adjustments you need to make in the upcoming months to upgrade and fine tune your lifestyle. Stay resourceful and adaptable and know that I am very proud of you for trying to live a high performance lifestyle. Good luck!

The Ten Rules of High Performance Living

Simplify Your Life

THE FIRST RULE to achieving High Performance Living is "Simplify Your Life." Simplifying starts with knowing how to recognize what in your life has the greatest value. It embraces what it takes to acquire, preserve, fortify, sustain, and protect what is most valuable. For example, your body, your mind, your soul, and your heart, in essence your health, all have priceless value. Your love relationships, your work relationships, and your lifestyle tell the story of your life.

The idea is simple, sane, and sound. Simplifying your life is the opportunity to address and meet your most personal needs with the intent to create a balanced, purposeful lifestyle. Be prepared to take the full responsibility to know:

- yourself
- your needs
- your priorities

To simplify, you will need to get the clutter and confusion out of your life. This is an important realization. In this simple process of cleansing, you come to terms with the emotional distractions, fears, weaknesses, and stumbling blocks that devalue your life. Purging any chaos and overload you experience will naturally simplify your lifestyle. In other words, simplification is an intelligent choice to enrich the quality of your life. It is imperative for lasting wellness.

To Simplify or to Self-Abuse

Not simplifying your life is conducive to disorder and confusion. In time, such chaotic living leads to a lifestyle of self-abuse. This is the most nefarious kind of abuse because it is easy to misdiagnose. Self-damaging behavior is the very opposite of simplification. Here, you beat yourself in the game of life and sabotage your own patterns of success.

When you do not answer to the task of simplifying your life, you are out of sync with your highest priorities. This sets the stage for stressful upheaval and unnecessary complications. Life is an ongoing challenge. There is enough pain and suffering in the normal growth cycles that lead to happiness. Why hassle and burden yourself with unnecessary pain and suffering? Too much suffering from prolonged adverse circumstances dampens the immune system and accelerates your aging. This will keep you from experiencing the full passion and beauty in being alive! Living a topsy-turvy, helter-skelter, jumbled life is like shooting yourself in the foot. You cannot feel great, look great, or experience enduring fulfillment when your behavior or belief systems are self-destructive.

Carly's Chaos

"Doctor, I've had it. I can't take it anymore! I wake up tired and go to bed exhausted. I am a bundle of nerves. I have no time for myself," Carly's voice rang out in desperation. "My life gets so stressed that I go into a state of panic. I can't even find the time to eat one meal a day in peace. No one told me. I had no idea what it was like to be a full-time mother, hold down a full-time job at the bank, and have two small children at home. I am thirty-seven and feel like I'm sixty. My work never ends. God knows I love my family more than anything else. My husband's job is stressful too. We never have time for just each other anymore. I'm not getting the emotional support I need. We're so tired at night that at best, we have sex once a week."

"There has to be more to this world than shopping, doing laundry, working, preparing meals for a fatigued husband, and taking care of the kids. The weekends are taken up with the kids soccer games and taking care of our elderly parents. We're both working, and together, we are barely able to pay our monthly mortgage. After the kids go to bed, I spend time studying and preparing for my real estate license. To top it all off, I got a call yesterday from my gynecologist. He told me they found an abnormal lump on my mammogram. What am I to do?"

A complete and thorough assessment of Carly's immune system, metabolism, and body chemistry led me to diagnose emotional burnout with anxiety and depressive components. This was accompanied by cystic mastitis (an inflammatory breast condition). Carly used to be an athlete in high school, but now she was stuck and sedentary. I told Carly she needed to simplify her life according to her highest priorities. Otherwise, the joy in her life would pass her by, just like the joy in her current life was blocked out. "Simplify your life and evolve with dignity or be at risk for having an unhappy and unhealthy life as you grow older."

Carly came to realize after studying the simple lessons in this chapter that her family, her health, and her children had the most value to her. She was able to see that adjustments were necessary in order for her and her husband to have more time for themselves to stay well and emotionally nourish each other. She recognized that this was more important than having more money. Carly simplified her life. She made time for her priorities, and in the process, she was true to her needs. She became a student of the Ten Rules of High Performance Living. Within three months, she was feeling herself again, and her breast lump had disappeared.

The names are different, the people are different, and the circumstances are different, but the story is virtually the same, "There has got to be more to life than this!" Yes, there is! Life is continually changing and so are we. Just as the seasons change, cycles in our life come and go. Success in one stage of our life does not guarantee success in future stages. We are not adolescents, teenage lovers, young adults, dads, or grandmas forever. But, we are forever needing to keep abreast with our roles and responsibilities in a world of extremes and rapid social and technological change. Whether it is about a relationship, a career, your health, or a place to live, getting what you want in life can be elusive. There is only one way to discover, acquire, and enjoy what you want, and that is to simplify your life!

Simplifying your life is finding out:

• what makes you happy
• what makes you tick
• what turns you on

This important health secret is known to those who stay fit for life. Simplifying your life is the solution to job dissatisfaction, relationship stress, and complications in your lifestyle.

Benefits

The great advantage to simplifying your life is that it brings the important things in your life into focus. It empowers you to focus on your soul, wellness, love, and family relationships. It teaches you to concentrate on job fulfillment and your purpose in life.

Simplification energizes your life. It toughens your mind, enlivens your heart, invigorates your spirit, and stimulates your body. This is why it is such a powerful and refreshing tonic to strengthen your immune system. Furthermore, it guides you to find the time to eat well, exercise, and have more fun. This creates balance and sound living habits.

When you simplify, your quality of life improves while you minimize stress and self-abuse. Simplifying puts you in the powerful position to gain closure on the most personal issues in your life. For example, you can rise to the occasion to marry, parent, succeed in business, or excel in sports, and yet, you are not standing in your own way to be fully alive and kicking. Additional benefits enable you to:

- Attune to your real feelings and thoughts
- Discover what you love to do
- Determine what is right for you
- Own the responsibility for your circumstances

You will love being alive and becoming inspired to realize the fulfillment inherent in a high performance lifestyle.

Richard's Burnout

Richard, a successful, well-educated thirty-seven-year-old banker came into my office complaining of low energy, fatigue, weight gain, and an increase in his blood pressure. His doctor told him that he was on the road to becoming diabetic and wanted to prescribe blood pressure medication. "I'm concerned about the effects the blood pressure medication will have on my sex life," said Richard, "since I already don't have the energy to keep on top of my nature as it is."

Richard's father had just had open-heart surgery, and yet, Richard still followed the traditional American diet, which consists of eating foods high in fat, protein, and refined sugars. His living habits were of great concern to me. He used alcohol, caffeine, and sugar for pick-me-ups throughout the day. He was addicted to stress and was becoming a workaholic. Worst of all, he was in denial of all this. He did not have the time to exercise and described his stress management program as "hit and miss." He was extremely frustrated about his work and his love relationships. He was severely pessimistic about his financial future because of a series of bad investments. "My wife cannot understand," he stated, "we already have two kids, and I don't think we can afford more right now. I used to think I had a bright future, and now, I'm not so sure." Richard was trying to keep up with his life, feeling more like the nail than the hammer.

Further discussions with Richard proved him to be suffering from the poor man's syndrome: He was poor in spirit, companionship, love, time, and health. Three or four times a year, he would get the flu or an upper respiratory infection and catch whatever was going around in his office. He was getting a bad attitude, and this was not helping his mental or physical health. All in all, he was overworked, overstressed, undernurtured, and nutritionally abused.

Interestingly, except for his blood pressure, diabetic, and weight concerns, the rest of his complete physical and laboratory tests were within normal limits. I diagnosed him with advanced burnout, a condition that traditional doctors neglect to diagnose. This meant his nervous system was being drained and his glandular system was being depleted. I explained to him that burnout with fatigue as its cardinal manifestation is a stepping stone to other degenerative illnesses like accelerated aging, heart disease, arthritis, cancer, stroke, liver disease, multiple sclerosis, and Alzheimer's disease. Richard said that the fear of future illness had no bearing on him since he was consumed with getting unstuck at home and at work.

Richard unconvincingly told me, "If I only had more time and money, I'm sure I could get it together." When I reviewed his medical profile with him, I made it abundantly clear that he was losing out on the most important areas of his life. His love relationship was slowly deteriorating. He was not happy. He was physically out of shape. His mind was negative. His emotions were suppressed, his spirit was low, and his immune system was depressed. He was not in control of his life.

I asked Richard who was causing his burnout, what was causing his burnout, and what were the benefits he was gaining from being diabetic, hypertensive, and burned out? Richard looked at me as if I was crazy, but within a few minutes, he came up with some answers. "Doc, I'm tired of being tired and letting my life spin out of control. I suppose my job is causing my tiredness, but I am a perfectionist and drive myself to work very hard. The only benefit I can think of is that there is no benefit. I want to feel better, but how do I do it, and where do I start?"

I told Richard that the benefit of his burnout was a wake-up call to study the Ten Rules of High Performance Living.

I told him, "Richard, illness is not something that is coming from the outside and getting into the body and attacking you. As an individual, you play a major role in your own self-created movie. Richard, you are leading a life of overload and confusion. You are what you eat and think and become what you believe and do. An individual is totally and fully responsible for their wellness and their health. Those people who are healthy, just like those in society who are successful, have created the habits of success and created their abundant lifestyle. Similarly, the people who are not well generally have not taken full responsibility for choices regarding nutrition, fitness, attitude, or self-awareness. Your self-abuse has dulled your senses and your feeling for life!"

I also explained to Richard that simplification was his first step in creating a lifestyle that is life-enhancing instead of self-destructive. I got through to Richard, and fortunately, he believed in my work. Richard took the program to heart. He began to look within. He decided that his health and his family were the most important things in his life. Within six weeks, he transferred into a different department, enabling him to work a forty-hour week. He made time for his wife and children. He made an important attitudinal adjustment about not wanting success at the expense of his health and happiness. He underwent a strict nutritional detox, lost forty pounds, and within six months, he lowered his blood pressure without the use of drugs. His blood sugar became normal without any chemical evidence of diabetes. He brought playfulness and a sense of humor back into his life. He rekindled his interest in jogging. He is now a happily married, forty-two-year-old banker staying on his path of light.

People often run on a treadmill of day to day tasks out of a sense of obligation, duty, or necessity. While adult responsibilities do exist, simplifying your life is a step toward creating harmony within yourself and with those around you. This way, you can enjoy what you determine to be of most value in your life. Focus on your true needs, and your priorities will allow you to understand the patterns and motives of your behavior. This will enable you to shed the habits that keep you running on that treadmill.

Your life is simplified when you know what you want. Knowing what you want is a start. More importantly, to simplify your life, it is imperative to get to know yourself better and determine what you need to be happy. Once you know what you need, spend more time within and bounce your ideas off those you respect to determine how to meet those needs. When you do not know what you need, you cannot possibly get it! When you do not know who you are, it is difficult to find out what you need.

Time for Action

It is now time for you to find out how to simplify your life. The following interactive section will guide you and teach you how to do it. Be sure to answer these questions from your heart center and not with what sounds like the right answer.

The keys to simplifying your life are:

- Look within for the answers.
- Become familiar with your uniqueness.
- Embrace the full responsibility for creating happiness and wholeness in your life.
- Know yourself: get in touch with your needs and priorities.
- Commit to being a self-sufficient, self-reliant, whole, happy person.
- Design a daily wellness plan to build strength, and create a daily health habit.
- Let go of the dead weight, and eliminate the clutter in your life.
- Avoid self-abuse.

Look within for the Answers

One important way to get to know yourself is to get in touch with what you love to do. As you get to know yourself, you can go in the direction of what really turns you on. Doing what you love nourishes your soul and keeps you young and spirited.

You can define who you are by the kinds of experiences that have the most meaning in your life.

What gives you total joy?

What kind of joys do you carry with you from childhood?

Adolescence?

Early romance?

What has been the peak emotional experience of your early or mature adult life?

Who is your hero?

Who has made the greatest impression in your life?

The fond memories that stand out or linger on give your life direction. At those very special moments, this is the real you. Listen to this voice in your heart! Your mind can have conflicting voices, but your heart speaks the voice of truth. Choose to listen!

Open your heart! Knowing who you are is getting to know what you feel from the bottom of your heart. Then pursue your inner loves. In doing so, you will simplify your life.

Find Your Inner Voice

Matters of importance that touch your heart also touch your soul. By feeling the message of your soul, you will know more clearly what is right for you. In knowing yourself, you will learn to recognize the truth of your inner voice.

In the silence of deep prayer and meditation, you will find yourself. Spending quiet time alone with nature helps you get in touch with your feelings. These are some of the most precious moments in your life. Allow yourself fifteen minutes alone in the morning and fifteen minutes in the evening in silent prayer and meditation (see chapter 8). Concentrate your mind, put a smile in your soul, and purify your heart. Ask yourself in the deep silence of your meditation

- What is my dominant mood?
- Am I really happy and fulfilled?
- What am I feeling?

The answers will be revealed in time.

Who knows you better than yourself? Who knows what is best for you? Who knows what is true for you? You do! You are blessed with a guiding inner voice. The inner voice of your soul is direct feedback that tells you what is right for you. Your inner voice is hidden by chaos.

Your inner self knows the truth when you hear it. When you listen to a song that smacks of truth, you know it. When you read a poem that has a ring of truth, it touches you. When you have a peak experience, you feel fully alive.

Become Familiar with Your Uniqueness

The gift of getting to know yourself is the magic of discovering your real identity. Take a few moments to write a short paragraph describing your personality. Be sure to list your strengths and weaknesses. It is also your responsibility to become clear about your personal values. What means more to you than anything else in your whole life?

The following paragraph was written by a patient, Mary Jane, who had suffered with migraine headaches for fifteen years. She was literally torn between what was best for her husband, her child, and her mother who lived with them. Getting her to think about herself or find out what she was feeling was a monumental task in facilitating her healing process. A week went by before she returned to my office with the following paragraph in hand.

"I am an intelligent, sensitive, searching romanticist and idealist. I'm in love with excitement, adventure, and helping others. I want to live for today, but I am always planning for the future. I am plagued with my headaches. I love to talk about nutrition, health, sex, athletics, and fitness. I love to feel needed. I realize that my greatest weakness is disorganization. I never seem to have enough time to do what I want to do. I seem to be hung up on pleasing my mother, daughter, and husband."

Mary Jane studied the simplification techniques in this chapter. She resolved her family conflicts by accepting herself and prioritizing her well-being in addition to her loved ones. Along with a high performance nutritional program, extra vitamin B-2, and feverfew herbal therapy, her migraines disappeared.

You could understand yourself more completely by discovering what you like and what you dislike. What is your opinion of the most common, everyday things in life, from traffic jams to TV commercials, arts, theater, music, and fashions to political or current events? What kind of people do you like to spend time with? Do not get frustrated when you are not sure what it is that you want to do with your life. For most of us mortals, we know for sure what we really do not want before we even begin to know what we do want, let alone what we need. By knowing what you do not like and do not want, you narrow down the choices in life. It helps you avoid going down blind alleys. How can you be true to yourself when you do not know who it is that you are trying to be true to?

Embrace the Full Responsibility for Creating Happiness and Wholeness in Your Life

You have the ability to respond to what is happening in your life; to care for yourself, nourish yourself, to value who you are. Emotional self-awareness, therefore, is the key to simplification. Allow yourself to get in touch with what really inspires you, and you will find out what you really need in life. For example, everyone needs to love and be loved. Everyone needs a positive self-image. Everyone needs to work their physical body, and everyone needs to have a purpose in life. This will transform the mystery of your life into the miracle of your life.

What patterns or themes keep repeating themselves? (relationship breakdown, poor health, financial worries, job burnout, sex concerns, etc.)

What do you need in your life to be fully happy?

What is your optimal dream come true lifestyle? Describe in detail.

What will it take to achieve this optimal dream?

Describe in detail what is optimal for you in your work or career.

What will it take to see this through?

Describe in detail what would be optimal for you in your primary love relationships?

What can you do to make sure this happens?

Balance Your Needs and Priorities

To simplify your life, your lifestyle must be patterned to satisfy your most fundamental needs and your most basic priorities. When your needs are met and your priorities are in order, your life is simplified. When your needs are not met and you spend time neglecting your priorities, your life turns to stress, chaos, and disorder. When your needs and priorities are in balance, you have discovered one of the secrets to lasting High Performance Living. When you spend most of your time working and accumulating finances, do not be surprised when your health or your relationships break down. Be certain that your foremost priorities get the most attention or, at the very least, enough attention. Outline specifically from top to bottom what the highest priorities in your life are:

1)

2)

3)

4)

5)

6)

7)

Others:

Is there any one area that weighs so heavily on you that you neglect your highest priorities?

What can you do to change this?

Commit to Being a Self-Sufficient, Self-Reliant, Whole, Happy Person

By getting in touch with your heartfelt commitments, you will discover the essence of your character. Your commitments are the actions that define who you really are and what you value most. What percentage of your life are you willing to commit to finding happiness and fulfillment? How committed are you to the disciplines of sound nutrition, meditation, and fitness? How strong is your commitment to your loved ones and your family? Do you stand up for what you believe no matter what?

It is important to realize that wellness is a prerequisite to sustaining high performance at work, home, or at play. High performance requires energy, concentration, and involvement. Unless you are well, it is not possible for you to realize your full potential. A commitment to High Performance Living and high performance relationships simplifies your life. It empowers you to reach your goals and live out your dreams.

Design and Organize a Sound Daily Wellness Plan to Build Strength and Create Order and Rhythm in Your Life

Design, organize, and adhere to a daily wellness plan to create balance and inner strength. A sunrise cleansing and a sunset recharge are vital to your program.

Sunrise Cleansing

Refreshing your mind, strengthening your body, opening your heart, and firing up your soul *in the first hour of the day* is the essence of Sunrise Cleansing. Start with exercise for at least twenty minutes upon awakening. Get up, get active, and breathe deeply. Choose a form of exercise you enjoy. After exercise, comes hydrotherapy. This means to immerse yourself in a natural body of water such as the ocean, a river, or a stream, or swim in a pool or take a cold shower. This activates your brain chemistry. After this, engage in a positive-thinking, heartfelt meditation for at least fifteen minutes. After meditation, get ready for a wholesome breakfast. By the end of the first hour, you will be a clear, vibrant channel of light and love. Expect an increase in happiness and vitality that will prepare you for the day.

Sunset Recharge

Late in the afternoon or ideally after work, between 4:30 and 7:30, spend at least twenty minutes exercising. The idea is to create a mind/body connection. You can do this while you are working out, or you can choose some form of yoga, t'ai chi, or kung fu. The key is to make time to recharge with a mind/body discipline before sunset when possible, but always before dinner. Follow the exercise with a fifteen minute meditation period. The Sunset Recharge will increase awareness and your energy for the evening. The third recharge of the day occurs naturally when you get a good night's sleep.

The energizing effects of the Sunrise Cleansing generally last six to eight hours. That is why it is best to recharge late in the afternoon to avoid drowsiness and fatigue. In the natural rhythm of going from a Sunrise Cleanse to a Sunset Recharge to a restful sleep, you gain harmony with yourself and the day. The result is an effortless flow of spirited energy. This simplifies your life.

Your timing and rhythm each day can either favorably or unfavorably influence the workings of your inner biological clock. Sound rhythm and natural timing nourish your physiology and lead to immunological competence. Dysrhythmic, dysfunctional, disorganized living impairs the immune system.

Sunrise Cleansing and Sunset Recharging are based on how your whole body works together:

Your body is the rechargeable battery. Exercise and feed it properly for strength, flexibility, and cardiovascular fitness.

Your emotions are the magnet. Positive energy attracts positive energy! Unload heavy, dark feelings and tensions, because fear and self-destructive thinking become self-fulfilling prophecies. Generate heartfelt love, and watch love and happiness come into your life.

Your mind is the transformer. Positive mental thinking is of key importance. Work with convictions and affirmations that encourage attitudinal healing. Believe in yourself, and sustain high self-worth.

Your spirit is the electricity. Meditation and time with nature and the outdoors allow for spiritual rejuvenation. Stay connected with yourself, others, and your environment.

Nature is very orderly, very harmonious, and very balanced. This wellness plan will to help you be that way too. It is up to the individual to take the responsibility to be whole, to bring order, and to bring balance into his or her life. Be sure to make an appointment with yourself at sunrise and at sunset so you can discover how great you really can feel every day!

In between your recharging intervals, focus on creating balance and productivity. Get involved in making tomorrow better than today and the day after tomorrow better than tomorrow.

Make a Decision to Let Go of the Dead Weight and Overload of Unnecessary Obligations

Make a list of all deadweight, unnecessary responsibilities, unneeded obligations, or self-abusive thoughts or behavior that overload you:

Home

Work

Relationships

Thoughts

Behavior

Now you know how to simplify your life. Before moving on to the next rule for High Performance Living, write in one hundred words or less what it will take to simplify your life. Be prepared to cleanse and make plans to simplify. Stick with your plans.

In principle, get to know yourself, get to know your needs, and focus on your priorities. Initiate the habit of daily wellness through exercise, emotional fitness, positive thinking, nutrition, and meditation. Through your daily habit of wellness, create rhythm and order in your life. Allow yourself to see the positive side to what life offers, then plan to experience it! In essence, simplify your life!

Lighten Up Your Life

THE SECOND RULE to achieving High Performance Living is "Lighten Up Your Life." Lightening up your life centers your personality around being lighthearted, fun-loving, and easygoing. It calms your mind and lightens up your thinking. It involves unloading the heaviness of unresolved emotional stress and letting go of bodily tensions.

The opposite of keeping it light is to wear the heaviness of emotional stress. This heaviness burdens the heart, weighs down the spirit, strains the mind, and dulls the senses. Emotional distress leads to burnout and fatigue. It is destructive to your immune system and erodes your health.

Relaxation in mind and body is the prescription of choice to lighten up your life. From a practical point of view, this means learning how to manage, reduce, and cope with the stress and strain of modern day living. Keeping it light empowers you to appreciate and enjoy every moment of your life. It makes more room for positive living. Additional benefits include:

- Balancing and energizing your life
- Enhancing your mental and physical performance
- Increasing your sensitivity to your most intimate feelings
- Increasing your sensitivity to others
- Improving your power of concentration
- Enlivening your soul
- Teaching you to recognize and release the burdens in your life
- Improving your ability to make sound decisions
- Giving you the power to simplify your life
- Connecting you to your all-knowing inner voice

Lightening up your life requires a cleansing of mind, body, heart, and soul. Cleansing the mind shines up your thinking and fortifies a positive mental attitude. Emotional cleansing empties the negative baggage that accumulates from bottling up your feelings and fears. It also opens and purifies your heart. Cleansing of your soul invigorates your spirit and brings the light in your life into focus. Bodily cleansing discards chemical toxins and eliminates unwanted poisons that build up from faulty eating habits. All these strategies help you purge unwanted stress.

Stress

Just as keeping it light is conducive to High Performance Living, accumulated prolonged stress is the leading cause to disease. Stress is the burdensome state of body overload. It does not feel good to be rushed, hassled, anxious, abandoned, or apprehensive. Emotional stress overloads your circuits. It results when your thoughts and feelings overreact to stressful life events. Excessive prolonged emotional and mental stress becomes emotional distress. In time, excessive levels of stress create a breakdown in the body's defense mechanisms.

In fact, the High Performance Living formula is based on the following equation:

$$\text{wellness} = \frac{\text{nutrition}}{\text{stress}}$$

Wellness is the high performance of your mind, body, heart, and soul. Nutrition is concerned with how well you take care of yourself; good food, good times, good friends, good fun, good loving are all important components of your personal nutrition. Your personal nutrition is enhanced by stopping to smell the roses and enjoying the wonders of sunshine, wind, mountains, rivers, and all natural elements. A balanced lifestyle is very nutritious. Emotional stress is a common form of self-abuse. The recipe to generate great health, vitality, and high performance is to practice more self-care and reduce the amount of stress you have in your life.

Stress can be experienced during adjustments or changes in your personal, social, working, or living conditions. The life event itself that triggers the stress is the "stressor." Your exaggerated reaction to the stressor is the "stress." You create your own levels of stress by how well you react to the stressors in your life. You are under stress when you overreact to life's circumstances without an appropriate release. Wellness is the positive state of being, where you adapt or respond to expected or unexpected changes in a relaxed, centered way. Wellness converts your stressful life events into opportunities for growth and healing. In other words, we all create our own levels of stress. You have a choice between creating wellness or destructive emotional stress by how well you cope with the challenges and threats to your well-being. Keep in mind that life is an endless myriad of inevitable changes. Whether or not your adult responsibilities become a heavy load in your life is entirely up to you.

Stress, then, is the lack of harmony between you and what is happening in your life. It is the heavy tax you pay for not taking responsibility in your life. In point of fact, any life event, experience, or interaction that throws you out of balance creates the wear and tear of daily stress.

Stressful life events take place in everybody's life. At one point or another, everyone faces the challenge of sustaining happiness. The responsibility of a new job, unfamiliarity of a new living environment, or the loss of love relationships are forces to be reckoned with. The birth of a child and the financial realities of raising your children and providing the best for your loved ones and family are parts of becoming a mature adult. Whether or not these changes become a heavy load in your life is entirely up to you. By taking responsibility for your life, you can convert your stress into opportunities for growth and healing. You can create wellness out of healthy stress levels, or you can go under from destructive levels of emotional stress. Being in control of your day to day stress, rather than controlled by it, is the essence of keeping it light. *Keeping the appropriate balance between fulfillment and stress is one of the secrets to lightening up your life.*

For example, say you find out that you may lose your job or you go to the parking lot and find you have a flat tire. What if your car breaks down on the freeway just before an important appointment? How do you deal with this?

Joe wakes up late. He cuts himself shaving and eats his breakfast on his way out the door. He puts on two different colored socks, tears his underwear while getting dressed, and mutters, "I'll never be late again." He thinks out loud and says that his whole day is ruined. He drives to work uptight, thinking he is going to lose a big account. He hates to rush but gets stopped by an officer for speeding.

Carrie wakes up late. She looks around and sees that it is a beautiful day. She is happy to be alive. She decides to cut her morning workout short and calls the office to inform them she will be late. She sits down to eat some fruit for breakfast, stays relaxed, and keeps things in stride. She heads to work with a positive mental attitude, looking forward to her day.

Ned is behind a slow truck on a one-lane highway. He screams, honks his horn, and grinds his teeth. He curses and works himself into a dander because he is late. Rex is mellow in the rush hour traffic jam. He gets behind a slow truck, practices some deep breathing exercises, and puts on his favorite cassette while he cruises down the highway.

It rains the day of the picnic, you cannot get the loan you want, you do not have enough money to get all your Christmas presents. Keeping it light teaches you to react calmly to the daily twist of events in your life. All too often, you stress out and become uptight. Anxiety and frustration create physical tension.

The habit patterns you develop for short-term stressful events are very significant. Short-term stressors turn up every day when you cannot find your wallet or keys, matching socks, or some important documents. The way you choose to respond will determine whether or not short-term stressful events become detrimental punches of emotional distress. Your response to the short-term stressors eventually becomes the habit pattern you develop to deal with heavy long-term stresses at home and at work. In time, little stress habits become big stress habits.

Michelle was a negative thinker suffering from blurred vision. I diagnosed her with stress-related high blood pressure. She did not exercise and had a diet high in animal protein, dairy products, and refined sugars. "Doctor, I may have high blood pressure," she claimed, "But I would not be here today if I weren't made out of cast iron." She added, "My husband never feels good. He's always sick with emphysema, and it's hard to be around him. The doctors told us to move away from the seashore, so we are selling our house and business property. Everything is going wrong. The escrow is being held up over a dispute for the last five months, and right now I am involved in a three million dollar lawsuit. I feel like a ton of bricks has fallen on me."

I asked Michelle "Do you realize that emotional distress is the single most common cause of bodily stress and dysfunction?" I commented that short-term negative thinking patterns become chronic negative thinking patterns. Before you know it, a few negative responses during each day become chronic worry, frustration, and anxiety. Exaggerated emotional responses with negative, pessimistic thinking develop a fatal pathway to chronic emotional distress. In Michelle's case, this was at the root of her high blood pressure. "Chronic anxiety burns out your nerves, your glands, and your hormones," I explained, "and it's a sure way to lose the game of life." I added, "You can also choose to nurture your mind and body with the positive habits of living. Make a habit of choosing positive, loving feelings and upbeat thoughts. Overload of your circuits with emotional stress and prolonged chronic mental strain becomes a part of you. Emotional distress in the context of chronic negative head trips is the basis for stress-related psychosomatic illness. Create psychosomatic health as an alternative to psychosomatic illness."

Your Target Organs Speak Out

Every human being has one or two target organs that are vulnerable to stress. These target areas are the parts of the body that cave in to stressful living. In other words, your target organs are your weak spots, your most sensitive parts, and the parts that manifest the signs of stress. Each individual's target organs are based on their own genetic engineering, metabolic individuality, and coping skills.

Every time Mary gets stressed out, she gets bronchitis. Every time Harry, a busy physician, gets upset about the mishaps in his busy schedule, he gets a backache. When J.B. worries about his marital separation, he gets indigestion. Keep in mind that your level of wellness will influence the threshold of negativity needed to fire off your most sensitive parts. A person who practiced sound nutrition, good health, and keeping it light could sustain much higher stress levels before their symptoms of target organ dysfunction would appear.

In addition, blocked feelings can also create uncomfortable stress levels in your target organs. Lightening up your life gets you in touch with your feelings. Your feelings are your most valued possessions. High performance living involves the creative self-expression of your innermost feelings. When Shelly found out that she was running away from her feelings, she straightened out her life.

See Shelly Run

Shelly was a stately, well-dressed thirty-nine-year-old marketing director. She had a slender frame, a warm smile, and curly red hair. She visited my office one lazy August afternoon because she was having abdominal spasms. These were accompanied by intense diarrhea—up to six or seven bowel movements a day. The abdominal cramps had been going on for three days, and she was feeling lousy. My first impression was that she had an intestinal virus, so I treated her conservatively with papaya-banana smoothies, soy yogurt, steamed carrots, and steamed zucchini. I advised her to drink peppermint and spearmint herbal teas in addition to taking warm baths and placing a castor oil pack over the lower abdomen for ten minutes when she got out of the tub.

When the spasms and diarrhea continued for the next seven days, I did a more thorough investigation. X-rays showed no evidence of cancer, ulcer, or diverticulitis. Stool specimens for blood and parasites were repeatedly negative. Ten more days passed, and she continued with spasms and diarrhea. I then diagnosed Shelly as having a spastic colon, a commonly used term for irritable bowel syndrome. The spasms in the colon are worsened by high levels of emotional stress.

I learned that Shelly had just had a falling out with her best friend. A quarrel had ended a close twelve year relationship. Shelly and her best friend, Phyllis, had both been divorced for six years. They lived on the same floor in an apartment complex overlooking the ocean. Phyllis had just ended a three year relationship with Paul. Shelly and her boyfriend, Mark, had been seeing each other for four years. In the last years, they had all developed friendships.

I found out that Phyllis was leaning on Mark, Shelly's boyfriend, to get over her depressed feelings of breaking up with Paul. She began to confide in Mark because she had nowhere else to turn. Phyllis wrote letters to Mark telling of her hurts and disappointments. She also revealed that Shelly had her doubts about the longevity of the relationship with Mark—a topic Shelly and Mark had never discussed. Shelly innocently found the letter in Mark's pocket while doing laundry. When she read what Phyllis had said in the letter, she felt betrayed. A few days later, she began to have cramps and diarrhea. I explained to Shelly that it is common for people to have symptoms of digestive disturbances when they are going through some kind of life crisis; especially when their digestive tract is their target organ. Upon further investigation, I found out Shelly had a similar condition nine years earlier, when she was having marital problems with her first husband. When Shelly decided to leave Ohio and move to the West, she found out her husband had put the make on Kelly, one of her friends. Within a few weeks of coming to California, she began to have colon spasms and diarrhea.

I explained to Shelly that it was likely she was not taking responsibility for the conflicts in her life. I told her that in my experience, buried hurt and anger often surface as a spastic colon condition. "Shelly, the crises in your life are life-giving opportunities to help you grow. The turning points in your life test your ability to keep it light and sustain high performance, high quality living. The only limitations are the ones you place upon yourself. Age is no barrier to how much you change, grow, experience, or self-improve. There is always time for growth, healing, and self-attunement."

I wanted Shelly to get to know herself and her patterns so she could simplify and lighten up her life. I asked her to write out a biographical sketch of her childhood, her adolescence, early adult years (up to thirty-five), and mature adult years (after thirty-five). In one column, I had her review the major joys and triumphs during these periods. In the other column, she listed the major losses, traumas, emotional sufferings, and pains that these periods of life had brought her.

	Pains	Joys
Childhood		
Adolescence		
Early adult		
Mature adult		

I asked Shelly to find out if there was a pattern or some common reaction to her most unsettling experiences. After doing her homework, Shelly realized what she was running away from. She returned to my office three days later with a smile on her face, feeling much better. After thinking it over, she realized she cherished her relationship with her best friend Phyllis, and she wanted to stay close to Mark. She talked to Phyllis and Mark and shared that she had found the letter Phyllis had written to him. She told them both, first individually, then together, how much she was hurt that she felt she could no longer confide in her friend Phyllis. Mark appreciated the confrontation since he was feeling uncomfortable with Phyllis's advances. Phyllis apologized for her disrespect and assured Shelly and Mark that her friendship with them was important for her as well. Over the next few weeks, they worked out the differences, and together with a high fiber, low-fat, chemical free nutritional plan, Shelly's diarrhea stopped, and her spastic colon disappeared.

Lightening up your life and staying well is fortified by knowing how you react to challenges, conflicts, and problems in your life. Shelly learned how to confront her fears and take responsibility to lighten up her life. In studying the stress management strategies at the end of this chapter, you will learn to develop habits of calmness and relaxation that prevent emotional strain.

Relaxation

Relaxation is a way of life. It is a state of mind as well as a state of wellness. It is the joyful feeling of being completely free. The art of relaxation is the art of being calm in mind and body. Keep in mind that real relaxation is effortless. When you feel good about yourself without feeling any strain or stress, you can enjoy being relaxed. Relaxation is a requirement to experiencing high-level wellness. Exciting options open up when you are one with yourself and fully relaxed. Relaxation is that breakthrough feeling of having no expectations and yet enjoying the moment in its total depth and dimension. Knowing how to relax in mind and body is a prerequisite to becoming competent in your own self-healing and managing your own wellness program.

Relaxation must precede any serious form of concentration. To be successful in any focused, concentrated moment, you are intuitively relying on your ability to be relaxed so you can concentrate, be creative, and skillfully get the job done. Relaxation has an invigorating and rejuvenating influence on your nerves and your brain. When your body and mind are relaxed, your organs, your body chemistry, and your nervous system are harmoniously physiologically receiving a normalizing effect. Relaxation is our normal, natural state. More can be accomplished when relaxed than when one is uptight.

Marathon Man

Woody was a tall, thin young man. He looked smart, dressed well, and had a pleasant personality. He had jogging on his mind. "I can't afford the time to be sick. Ever since I ran the Honolulu Marathon, I haven't been the same man. I seem to tire more easily than before, and I'm usually wiped out before dinner time. But what really brings me here to you today, doctor, is that this is the third prostate infection I've had in six months. I've seen two other physicians who prescribed antibiotics, and I'm still not any better. Isn't there a more natural way to treat these infections?"

In taking his history, I found that Woody had run marathons in the past. His usual training included jogging five to six miles a day. In preparing for the marathon, he would work up to ten miles on the weekends and forty to forty-five miles a week.

Woody explained that he loved to do things he had never done before. He wanted to prove to himself that he still had what it takes. I scheduled Woody for a complete physical. I could find nothing physically wrong with his urinary tract. Since a series of prostate infections in a thirty-five-year-old man is unusual, I sent Woody for x-rays of his kidneys and bladder. While waiting for the results of his lab tests and x-rays, I asked Woody to keep a daily journal of how he spent his time, "Break down your day into morning, afternoon, and evening. Pay special attention to your moods, especially when eating breakfast, lunch, and dinner."

When I saw Woody in the office one week later, I informed him that all his x-rays and tests were normal. When I looked at his weekly journal, I was impressed with his own account of being uptight the great majority of the day. "I don't have enough time to do anything I want to do," Woody said. Woody was an architect by trade. "There is not enough time for me to get my work done at the office. I don't have enough time to spend with my wife, and whenever I am with her, she tells me that I am stressed. In fact, she is threatening to leave me unless I can get myself together. I barely have enough time to take care of my personal responsibilities, my car, or my checking account as it is. I need eight hours of sleep, and I seem to need more since I ran the marathon in Honolulu." Woody had acquired one habit to pacify his super anxious state. He would always reach for his favorite candy bar or sweet rich desserts to satisfy his levels of anxiety. After completing a thorough history and physical, I pointed out to him that being uptight and chasing the clock had become a way of life to him. Woody agreed that he did not know how to relax or fully unwind. He shared that his anxiety level drove him to be productive. Woody suffered with a common ailment that affects most successful professionals. Success and modern day chaos often means you pay a price by being over-stressed and out of touch with how to have fun and relax. The irony is that you can be most successful and productive when you are relaxed.

I explained to Woody that the key to relaxation was to make each moment of your life totally fulfilling in its own right. Then you can feel at home wherever you are and with whatever you are doing. I gave Woody some checkpoints so he could determine for himself if he was relaxed. You can use these questions to help you determine whether you are relaxed in whatever you are doing.

- Are you feeling lighthearted?
- Do you feel calm and peaceful?
- Do you feel a sense of inner joy in your heart?
- Do you feel like you are being yourself?
- Are you in touch with your true feelings?
- Are you happy to be where you are?
- Are you going at your own pace?
- Do you feel at home and good about yourself?
- Are you happy to be with the people you are with?
- Are you really cheerful?

When you can answer yes to the majority of these questions, you are relaxed. When you answer no, you are not relaxed.

Over the course of a few months, Woody studied the techniques and principles for lightening up your life. He learned to look within and get to know himself. He began to take responsibility for his life. With the help of a special alkaline nutritional detoxification and cleansing program, Woody did not encounter any further infections. In time, he learned how to relax and be himself.

When you are at ease with yourself, you are relaxed, happy, and in harmony with whatever you are doing. Keeping it light and staying in touch with the light in your life promotes relaxation.

It is important to trust your inner voice that tells you that you are comfortably at ease. It is very interesting how, in a state of full relaxation, you can be productive, while normally daunting tasks seem effortless. This is because you are doing what comes naturally, and you are in the right place at the right time.

When you do not feel that "down home" feeling of being one with yourself, the opposite of relaxation occurs. Restlessness means you are out of step with yourself and is the basis for anxiety. The habit of relaxation is learned from being at one with yourself. This harmony has two special ingredients:

- knowing who you are
- knowing what you love to do

Once you know these, it is easy to learn how to relax. When you are relaxed, you can comfortably and successfully deal with your life. When you relax, you are centered, peaceful, and able to cope with whatever is happening in your life. Learning how to relax precedes learning how to meditate, ski, heal yourself, play tennis, or anything that requires mind/body coordination. In fact, you have to be centered to heal yourself. It is the only way to keep grounded in the unpredictable winds of change. Relaxation is conducive to being centered.

Understanding how one can apply relaxation to achieve High Performance Living requires awareness of the three kinds of relaxation.

- Passive relaxation
- Creative relaxation
- Active relaxation

Passive Relaxation

Going to the movies, watching TV, getting a massage, taking a nap, or going to a ballgame are called passive forms of relaxation. They take you away from your daily routine and out of yourself. These modes of getting unwound usually do not involve any effort whatsoever and on these grounds alone are valuable.

Creative Relaxation

Creative relaxation can be even more important. The total mental and emotional involvement in writing, painting, composing, meditation, or playing a musical instrument re-channels your energy into relaxed productivity. This is healing therapy for your mind. Creative relaxation gives you a heightened sense of well-being.

Active Relaxation

In addition to passive and creative relaxation, other forms of more active relaxation come into play. Active relaxation is meditation in movement. It is involved participation in life, as opposed to being a passive spectator. In activities that are both mental and physical, such as jogging, yoga, swimming, dancing, exercising, lovemaking, or those physically adventurous times with your friends and loved ones, you can get the greatest benefits of relaxation. It is only through this active relaxation that you can gain entrance into knowing yourself.

Time for Action

It is now time for you to find out how to lighten up your life. The following interactive section will give you strategies and techniques to relax, reduce stress, and lighten up your life.

Learning how to prevent unnecessary emotional stress will move you forward on the path toward High Performance Living.

Your mind has a lot to do with effectively managing stress. Optimistic positive thinking is the mental formula for a healthy, happy life, especially in the face of crises. When you create positive solutions to your daily challenges, you prevent lots of unnecessary emotional stress. Negative thinking is destructive to your health and sets you up for a chronic stress pattern. Pessimistic, fearful, fatalistic, and hostile negative reactions to the tribulations and surprises in your life are a losing strategy.

Take Inventory of the Kinds of Stress in Your Life.

What kind of burden(s) do you believe you have at home?

What action steps can you take to resolve this?

What kind of burden(s) do you believe you have at work?

What action steps can you take to resolve this?

What kind of burden(s) do you believe you have with your financial matters?

What action steps can you take to resolve this?

What kind of burden(s) do you believe you have with your relationship with yourself?

What action steps can you take to resolve this?

It is your responsibility to make the changes in your attitude or circumstances to unload your emotional distress. Begin today and be consistent.

What about your thinking needs to lighten up? (i.e., chronic worry or guilt)

What about your feelings needs to lighten up? (unresolved anger, fears, or insecurities)

What about your body needs to lighten up? (i.e., your weight, tension in your neck)

Size up the main distractions and frustrations in your life. This will help you target what areas of your life need to lighten up. Ongoing emotional distractions and frustrations can be used as vehicles to find the light in your life. Otherwise, these distractions and frustrations can accumulate and cause more and more stress.

What are the main frustrations or emotional distractions in your life?

What action steps can you take to resolve this?

Learn to use stress management techniques to zap burnout and effectively reduce your stress levels. Keep in mind that what determines whether a stressful life event (stressor) becomes a distress is you! The most intensely stressful life events (divorce, death of a loved one, financial collapse, bad health, etc.) increase your susceptibility to illness. The greater the upheaval and the larger the loss, especially of sudden impact, the greater the potential for even more stress. A cluster of stressful changes can lead to chronic stress. In essence, the nature of your stress level will be determined by:

- the stressful life event
- unrealistic expectations
- your perception of the stressor
- your response
- your adaptability
- your vulnerability

Here's what you can do about it!

Stressful life event. The more responsibility you take for your life, the less things can go wrong. For example, when you do not take care of your car and maintain it properly, you can become easily stressed when it costs hundreds of dollars for avoidable repairs. The same thing can happen to your body and your relationships when you neglect them. People usually take better care of their cars and pets than they do of themselves. Many stressors can be prevented by skillful living. Start with being yourself. It is very stressful when you are not true to yourself, and it is very natural when you feel you can be yourself. This will prevent many unnecessary stressful life events at home and at work.

Adopt realistic expectations. Unrealistic expectations create a variety of unnecessarily stressful events. When you expect too much from others, they will often disappoint you. When you expect everything to be perfect, it will put you under enormous pressure. Realistic expectations help you achieve High Performance Living—keep your mind and body balanced. Become self-reliant. This will reduce what you expect others to do for you.

Your perception of the stressor. Learn to see the glass as half full instead of half empty. When you are insecure, ordinary life events can threaten you. See yourself as a winner, and you will take most life events in stride. A positive mental attitude will help you see things clearly. Establish a positive self-image, and nurture your self-esteem.

Your mind also interprets what is happening to the circumstances of your life. Reacting to stressors in an appropriate, intelligent way is a key element in the keeping it light strategy. In other words, your perceptions are vitally important because whatever you perceive to be a threat in your life will become a major life stressor.

In reality, there are fundamentally two things that can relate to every major life event. There is what actually happens and what you think is happening. Your wife tells you that your secretary is mismanaging your bookkeeping. You explode and say there is no way you will ever fire her. You feel your husband has been holding back from telling you his out-of-town, on-the-road activities. When he says he will be late for dinner, your most personal reactions and feelings of anxiety trigger indigestion. You think your boss is upset with you, and you worry about not getting a raise. You sit by the typewriter all day with a splitting headache. You perceive stress, and you will experience it. Myopic warped perceptions create emotional distress.

A positive self-worth and self-confidence prevents distorted perceptions. Your perception of reality is going to depend upon your past experiences, your sensitivities, values, and especially your own self-worth and self-respect. So what do you think happens when moderate to minor stressors are seen as threats to your security with your loved ones or your job? It is very clear what happens. You react inappropriately. Exaggerated emotional stress is then passed on to the involuntary autonomic nervous system to lower your immune system and cause disease.

- Do you see yourself as a winner or as someone unable to be happy? Marilyn concluded that she was unable to be happy, and with every passing adversity, she was convinced of a negative outcome. Her belief systems were so entrenched in fear that she went on to suffer with chronic allergies and asthma.
- Do you see yourself as unable to establish long-term, lasting relationships? That is how Megan saw herself. She moved from city to city looking for Mr. Perfect. Whenever she had a conflict with someone she was close to, she got scared, shut down emotionally, and could not work things through.

Changing the way you see yourself and valuing who you are will alter your levels of stress, because you can see the big picture and you will learn to take things in stride. How you see things determines how you respond. When you see yourself as a victim, you create unhealthy stress patterns. When you take responsibility for yourself and hold yourself in high regard, you can keep it light and handle your life's challenges with dignity and humor.

Your response to the stressor. Your coping skills have everything to do with whether stressful life events become growth-oriented experiences or destructive emotional stress. Creative constructive responses to daily stressors are conducive to inner strength, healing, self-preservation, and self-control. When you overreact or underreact to a significant stressor, it throws you out of balance. Learn to stay calm and take it easy.

Your adaptability to the stressor. There are a series of specific coping skills that enhance your adaptability. These coping skills foster internal equilibrium, increase your resistance to disease, and are the basis for an effective stress management program. The more resourceful and diversified your stress management plan, the less stress you will experience. Commit to a daily stress reduction program.

In your tool kit, you can find the following resources for self-regulating stress levels:

- a sound physical fitness program
- nutritional balance
- regular meditation
- creative self-expression
- self-nurturing activities
- fun and laughter
- friends and loved ones
- mind/body disciplines (yoga, t'ai-chi, kung fu)
- spiritual awareness
- emotional fulfillment

Your vulnerability to the stressor. Retained fear, suppressed anger, and buried hostility increase your susceptibility to over-reacting to stressful life events. Chronic worry, guilt, emotional dependencies and codependencies, and poor self-esteem often distort your perceptions and obstruct appropriate responses. Size up your fears of failure, rejection, and loneliness, and replace them with courage. Determine whether fear of abandonment or fear of intimacy is setting up addictive behavior. Identify your resentments and guilt, and replace them with forgiveness. Substitute love for anger. Cure chronic worry with an optimistic, positive mental outlook.

Acquire the Habit of Relaxation

Regular exercise will teach you how to relax physically. Daily meditation will show you how to relax mentally. Deep breathing exercises will help you unwind and let go. Learn to do one thing at a time with full concentration, and this will lead you to an automatic state of relaxation. Learn to live in the moment, "be here now," and this will relax your soul! Avoid borrowing problems from the past or worrying about the future. Learn to find your center, and stay in touch with your inner guides.

The habit of relaxation empowers you to let go of anxiety and restlessness. By getting in touch with the light and love in your heart, you can find inner joy and peace within. Regularly scheduled periods of meditation practiced at least two times a day for twenty minutes at a time will teach you how to create the peaceful feeling of relaxation. The secret is to be relaxed through whatever you do during the day. Regardless of the complexity of the task, use this formula to relax through the known, unknown, or unexpected crises in your life.

Dr. Barnet's Seven-Point Yield and Empty
Formula for Relaxation

1) Find a natural setting, sit with your back straight, and relax your physical body.

2) Quiet your mind. Experience the silence, and look within.

3) Identify with what you love the most. Inhale and expand with these feelings of inner joy as you...

4) Exhale, yield, and empty any tensions or anxiety in your mind or body. This will empty your mind. Continue to inhale and exhale in this fashion for at least five minutes.

5) Fully experience yourself in the moment, 100 percent involved in your breathing in love and exhaling stress.

6) Continue to let go of all bodily tensions until you feel centered.

7) Relax and creatively enjoy your divine bliss!

To master the habit of relaxation, come to terms with the following kinds of questions.

- What situations make you tense and make you feel uptight?
- What strategy can you take to prevent this?
- What are the main ways you know how to fully relax and have fun?
- How much time everyday do you spend fully relaxing/having fun?

- Do you have a relaxation deficiency?
- Do you have enough fun and laughter in your life?
- If not, what can you do about it today?

Keeping it light empowers you to unload the emotional stress in your life. Get in touch with the love and the light in your heart. Learn how to relax, and let go of anxiety, restlessness, and bodily tensions. Create a lifestyle of being calm and centered. In time, you will find that by being yourself, accepting yourself, and loving yourself, you will lighten up your life. Waiting for that special person to make the world right for you invites disillusionment. Stalling for that magical vacation or weekend to relax you is bound to limit your growth. You will become a slave to one restless activity after another. When your relationships or working conditions are not fitting into the scheme of your whole life, restlessness occurs.

Relaxation is something you want to be doing, because it fits into the scheme of your whole life. It is important to determine if an activity or project you undertake is an important link to your overall goal. Every worthwhile goal in life has its prerequisites or lifestyle requirements which are stepping stones to your desired reality. For example, to become a doctor, I had to go to medical school. Med school was boring at best, but I had to make the best of it. When a project is part of your chosen reality, accept it. Find out the most interesting features about it, and enjoy and relax into what you are doing.

In learning to relax, you must let everything go, both mentally and physically. There is a difference between letting go of short-term tension and long-term tension. Frictions with other people, disappointments, fleeting hatred and anger, mechanical failures of your car, washer, or TV, and loss of money are all short-term tension producers (stressors). Short-term tension is an unexpected weekend visit from your mother-in-law. It is "in the moment anxiety."

Letting go of long-term tension producers (stressors) requires mastering the habit of complete, continuous relaxation. A year of house reconstruction, a houseguest deciding to extend their visit for three months, marital separation, and the loss of a loved one all produce long-term tension. It is easier to let go and develop continuous relaxation when you attain self-acceptance. When you are relaxed, you are more comfortable with who you are and better able to successfully deal with your life. It will guide you to uncover states of emotional denial which may be hidden within. Relaxation leads to being centered, and you have to be centered to heal yourself. It is the only way to stay grounded in the unpredictable winds of change. In effect, mastering the habit of relaxation will teach you how to lighten up your life. Keep it light and be well!

Take Charge
of Your Life

"TAKE CHARGE of Your Life" is the third rule to achieving High Performance Living. Taking charge means taking command of your thoughts, intentions, actions, and deeds. It is all about being captain of your destiny. It is up to you to create a heartfelt, soul-filled love relationship with life. This means you are responsible for your own state of affairs, including your level of fulfillment or your degree of suffering.

Taking charge involves taking full responsibility for your success or failures, whether they be at home, in the boardroom, or in the bedroom. In studying the mind/body connection, the facts are well-established and undeniable. You have created whatever is happening in your life. The truth is, you have to answer to yourself.

Taking charge teaches you that you can choose to be the hammer rather than the nail. In fact, you are what you choose to think, feel, eat, and do. Taking charge is very practical and is goal oriented. You see, the purpose of taking charge of your life is to empower you with the tools to live out your dreams. Your beliefs, a positive mental attitude, clear thinking, and self-determination will be the key instruments in your tool kit.

Everybody has their own dream. It is your privilege to have the vision and own the power to see your dreams come true. You have the capability to change the course of your life. You automatically take charge of getting your food, providing shelter and warmth, and securing transportation. You would not expect someone to fill your refrigerator, do your shopping, or purchase your gasoline. Why then would you give the responsibility of creating your visions and fulfilling your dreams to someone else?

Develop a Winning Belief System

There is an intrinsic bridge between your belief systems and your life vision. To live your dream, it is up to you to develop a positive belief system that is oriented toward High Performance Living; wellness, success, and fulfillment. In taking charge, it is vitally important to get in touch with your feelings. Why? Because you become what you feel! Furthermore, your feelings shape your belief systems.

When you value yourself, respect yourself, and feel good about yourself, it is a simple matter to create positive, winning belief systems. In taking charge, it is crucial to believe in yourself, to believe in what you are doing, and to nurture the heartfelt belief that you deserve to be healthy and happy. When you love yourself, you can fully believe you deserve a fulfilling life.

When you enjoy the level of fitness, fulfillment, and happiness you desire, you can be certain you have developed healthy, positive belief systems. On the other hand, your life can become an endless roller coaster of disappointments, ups and downs, and failures. When life is not working out and you are not experiencing lasting prosperity at home, at work, or at play, consider that your fundamental reality is dominated by fear-oriented, self-destructive belief systems. It is common for negative belief systems to create patterns of behavior that actually keep you from reaching your ultimate goals.

Belief systems have a way of becoming self-fulfilling prophecies. With "take charge," positive belief systems, you can look forward to penetrating personal fulfillment, superior personal achievement, and enduring productivity. When fear dominates the way you feel, believe, and think, it gets in the way of your life. Fear of failure causes failure. Fear of abandonment creates abandonment, just as fear of intimacy causes relationships to break down. Fear of rejection breeds rejection. Fear of not being good enough creates emotional isolation, and so on and so forth. It is only when love and self-worth are central to how you feel about yourself that you will not sabotage your life.

This is why it is so important to spend time getting in touch with your real feelings about yourself. Do you love yourself? Do you respect yourself? Do you believe you deserve the best? Examine your feelings. Taste them, measure them, and then you will be in touch with your real beliefs. When you cannot keep a job, be assured that you do not believe you can. When your relationships fall apart every couple of years, realize that you do not believe it is possible for you to sustain a long-term, monogamous, passionate relationship. What could possibly be the advantage to having negative beliefs about yourself or life? Reprogramming your belief systems is at the core of healing yourself.

Her Beliefs Came True

I got the phone call the night before I was leaving for vacation. Crystal was calling from a downtown emergency facility. She sounded desperate, "Dr. Barnet, I'm at my wits end. I'm hemorrhaging from below. My uterus won't stop bleeding." I asked,

"Are you pregnant?" "No," she replied. Crystal was a thirty-seven-year-old, gorgeous, long-haired blonde. She was tall, had very clear skin, pretty green eyes, and the hands of an artist. She had been to see her gynecologist no less than three times in the last six weeks. He was treating her with progesterone hormone injections to temporarily arrest her irregular, but profuse hemorrhaging. Her doctor had informed her that unless she stopped bleeding, he would admit her the next day to do a diagnostic surgical procedure called a D and C (dilation and curettage) to find out the cause of her bleeding. "I am afraid of doctors, and I don't want surgery. There must be an alternative, Dr. Barnet. Can you help me?"

When I examined her in my office that evening, I could find nothing abnormal in the physical examination of her ovaries, uterus, or her cervix. I could detect no fibroids on her uterus or polyps on her cervix. She had one five-year-old daughter who was fine and born under normal conditions. In taking her medical history, I determined that Crystal had been under a great deal of tension for that last few years. She commented that she was trying to keep her family together, and for the past two years, she was supporting her husband while he was attending law school. She shared that she had not been happily married since her daughter was born. Recently, her father had been hospitalized with a stroke, and her sister had been diagnosed with high blood pressure. This present bleeding episode began two days after her in-laws, who had just filed for bankruptcy, moved in for a month. "I am a victim of these morbid circumstances," she stated.

Crystal had been feeling depressed and anxious for the past three months. Every day from 2 to 5 o'clock in the afternoon, she would feel awful and had a classic dietary abuse pattern. Typically, around 3:30, she would yearn for chocolate, sweets, root beer, or chocolate cream pies. She would give in to her cravings and feel absolutely miserable one hour later.

At least three times, she mentioned that she had been walking around with a feeling that disaster could strike at any moment. She had felt this way for most of the year. "Now," in her own words, "my time has come."

I determined that Crystal was suffering with a hormonal imbalance brought on by self-abusive, emotional, and dietary stress. Crystal felt trapped, guilty about possibly leaving her husband, and afraid to be on her own. At the crux of the matter was a very negative belief system about herself.

I explained to Crystal that the best way to balance her hormones was through a natural, non-drug, non-invasive approach. It is called adhering to the Ten Rules of High Performance Living. I explained to Crystal that her beliefs needed to be reevaluated since she did not believe in herself. I told Crystal that she needed to take charge of her life and, essentially, take charge of her belief systems. Crystal had programmed disaster into her life and was now faced with picking up the pieces. "Belief systems have a way of becoming a reality," I told her, "Are you ready for a change?"

I started Crystal on a raw food cleansing diet and instructed her to practice three healing meditations fifteen to twenty minutes before each meal. I instructed her to put her hands over her uterus and visualize the bleeding to stop as one would turn off a faucet that was leaking out of control. I advised her to channel her heartfelt loving feelings through her hands to heal her own body. "Positive belief systems unfold from natural instinctive loving feelings," I told her, "Negative belief systems are a defense mechanism. They are overcompensation for or overreaction to the emotional wounds you carry within you. These wounds create fears and in turn, self-destructive belief systems and addictive, self-abusive lifestyles."

In heartfelt meditation, you can get to the bottom of your belief systems. In a state of relaxation, allow your negative beliefs to surface. Examine them, evaluate their origin, and then make the conscious and clear awareness that they no longer benefit you. Authorize your intuitive, positive beliefs to take charge of your life. You cannot bury your old negative belief systems under the carpet. Indeed, you can reprogram them and replace them with positive, wellness-oriented belief systems.

Under my supervision, Crystal studied the Ten Rules of High Performance Living and began to take charge of her life. She got in tune with herself and began to resolve her emotional conflicts at home and with herself. She put together a new positive attitude along with a fitness, meditation, and high quality nutritional program. Over the next two to three weeks, Crystal's bleeding gradually disappeared. In fact, after five days of cleansing, there was only occasional spotting. In another two months, her menstrual cycle had completely returned to normal. One year later, she was still without menstrual dysfunction and was dutifully employed as a popular guidance counselor at a local university. Crystal's new beliefs were inspiring to everyone. They attracted happiness and fulfillment in her life.

Your Belief System and Your Immune System

Your belief systems have a hand to glove relationship with your immune system. Positive belief systems open the channels for creative healing energy to work. Nadine, for example, believes in the importance of nutrition. Whenever she feels a cold coming on, she starts on a cleansing diet, and the next day, she feels better. Ross is a great believer in physical fitness. Whenever he feels a little bit down, he dons his jogging shoes and exercises himself right out of it. Candy believes in the power of spirit. Whenever she feels out of balance, she meditates until she is centered. Jennifer believes in hatha-yoga. Whenever her sciatica acts up, she practices her yoga exercises, and shortly thereafter, her back pain disappears.

Certainly, positive beliefs favorably affect the optimal functioning of your body. Your belief systems have an influence on your autonomous or involuntary nervous system. Positive beliefs have a favorable affect on your neuroendocrine (nerve-hormone) system. Similarly, your beliefs of fear, inadequacy, and insufficiency are destructive to your immune system. Your belief systems reverberate throughout your body and vibrate in the amphitheater of your conscious and subconscious mind. That is why your beliefs can change your body chemistry. Your life is not only greatly influenced by what you believe in, but you are usually most successful at what you believe in the most.

Belief systems have infinite healing powers but work within the boundaries defined by the physical laws of the universe. You can believe that jumping off the Coronado Bridge is not going to hurt you, but this is obviously disrespecting the laws of gravity. You can believe junk food is good for you and still age rapidly. You can stand in front of a moving car and believe that you will not get hurt, but you will find that this is not so.

There is a big difference between the happy, healthy individual and the victim who is suffering from endless emotional turmoil and circumstantial stress. High Performance Living mandates living according to positive beliefs. Are you ready to accept this? When you surrender control of your health to random outside forces, you have essentially surrendered your belief systems and given away your power. When you believe that invisible germs are responsible for your illness, you are falling victim to your own self-neglect. Learn to rely upon yourself for your health, security, and well-being. Believe in yourself, and you will do very well. Be lax on your expectations about yourself, and your chronic self-doubt will become disappointment in time.

It is usually more comfortable to blame others for the adverse circumstances in your lifestyle. The path of least resistance is not always the best. The truth is, you have the power to take control of your life. There is no such thing as being a helpless victim: You are a victim only if you choose to allow yourself to be one. A victim gives his/her power away and allows society and others to manipulate them. You always have options; you simply need to exercise them. Remember, you are what you choose to think, feel, and do. Some common options are: the choice of positive or negative thoughts, happy or sad emotions, rewarding or destructive relationships, a nutritious or unhealthy diet. You also choose your goals, career, daily habits, friends, and lifestyle. Through these choices, you create wellness or illness, happiness or misery, success or failure. It is a simple matter to see yourself as a victim of circumstances, especially when you lack self-confidence and have a poor self-worth.

Your Self-Worth Counts

Your self-worth is determined by the way you really feel about yourself. Your self-image is how you see yourself and winds up being the deep-seated emotional opinion of your precious life. Taking charge of your life and building your self-esteem are inseparable. Becoming aware of your own magnificence invites your self-esteem to come alive. Since your feelings and thoughts about yourself determine how you act, your self-worth determines your behavior.

When you incarcerate your self-esteem, you feel different levels of being worthless. This devalues your life. When you have a negative opinion of yourself, you feel unworthy of love. In time, low self-worth invites rejection and failure. Until you develop a positive self-esteem with dignity, humor, and enthusiasm, your negative self-image will be an obstacle to your fulfillment and happiness.

A healthy self-esteem means you believe in yourself from deep down inside your soul, where it really counts. Your beliefs are the sacred keys that open the vault of understanding to your personality and behavior. When you sincerely believe that you are a worthy, special human being, this develops emotional self-confidence. Then, you can keep up with the challenges that life presents to you and can usually favorably handle whatever comes up.

Therefore, it is what you really believe about yourself that determines your self-worth. It is common for people to develop a belief system in life that they are either winners or losers. Victims live with the belief that they are losers and are comfortable with settling for less than they deserve. On the other hand, when you believe in yourself, you find it second nature to love yourself, have confidence in yourself, and value yourself. The creative constructive metamorphosis of changing from a negative to a positive belief system can be accomplished. It will require concentration of your thinking and the vivid picture power of your imagination. These tools will guide you as you prepare yourself to address the action steps in taking charge of your life.

How to Take Charge of Your Life

The following techniques are the keys to effectively taking command of your life.

- Embrace the responsibility for taking charge of your mind and body.
- Take charge of your thinking, and create the habit of a positive mental attitude.
- Be opportunistic.
- Be visionary and goal oriented.
- Gain self-confidence, and develop self-worth.

- Utilize willpower and self-determination to create the habit of success.
- Make the appropriate and necessary adjustments in your attitudes, beliefs, and expectations to stay in charge of your life.
- Be proud of who you are.
- Learn the mechanics of self-care.

Action Steps to Take Charge of Your Life

Take Responsibility!

How can you begin to assume control? The essential first step in taking command of your life is accepting full custody for your mind, body, and spirit. When you blame outside circumstances for your own situation, you thwart your own growth and actually cheat yourself. You are responsible! Commit to taking charge of your life. Make it a priority.

What areas of your life do you need to take full responsibility for that you currently delegate to others or have become codependent on others for? (i.e., health, happiness, sexuality, financial independence)

Take your life back, and face up to your responsibilities!

What circumstances in your life are not working for you?

Who is to blame for this?

What can you do about it today?

What symptoms of burnout or poor health do you currently have? (i.e., fatigue, indigestion, arthritis, back pain, menstrual dysfunction, depression, overstressed, anxiety)

For each symptom, describe:

Who is causing it?

Could it be you?

What is causing it? (consider nutritional or emotional abuse)

What is the benefit of having this problem?

Do you find comfort in avoiding responsibility for yourself and getting attention in a negative way?

Take Charge of Your Thinking

Taking charge of your life means taking charge of your thoughts. Mind power has everything to do with living out your dreams.

Your attitude and your expectations need to be transformed into a winning belief system.

Become an optimist, not a pessimist. Learn to think positively, especially in the face of adversity. Start with the little challenges and minor predicaments. Take charge of your thinking, and condition your mind to expect the best results. Learn how to think positively in a consistent fashion. When you are pregnant, expect a healthy baby. When you start a business, expect it to be successful. When you enter a new relationship, expect it to last. As you develop sound, positive habits of thinking, you will be able to successfully face up to any trying circumstance.

Be Opportunistic!

Seize the power within yourself, and do not give away your power to do what is best for you. When opportunity knocks, seize the moment. Be patient, and keep the faith; your moment in the sun will reveal itself. Do a good job at whatever you do, and keep an open mind for even better things to happen. Learn to enjoy and be involved in every moment of your life. Choose to make the best out of each situation. When opportunity arises, go for it! When you have the right attitude, it is uncanny how you can be in the right place at the right time.

Be Visionary and Goal-Oriented

Set your sights on discovering the fruits of High Performance Living; ecstasy, fulfillment, and happiness. Plant the seeds for success, prosperity, and wellness every day with a positive mental attitude. Follow through on a daily basis to enrich the quality of your life. Condition your mind to expect the best. Remember, your thoughts create actions. Create a dominant pattern of solution-oriented thinking. Determine the conflicts that exist in your life. Take the necessary steps to resolve them. Analyze the predicament clearly.

Describe your attitude and circumstances with respect to any unresolved conflicts with:

Loved ones

Family

Work and Career

Friends

Now take charge! The past does not equal the future. Realize that you have the mind power to transform your life through solution-oriented choices. Decide what is the solution to each of your predicaments, and take charge.

What is it that you have to face up to in the next three months? (i.e., job change, moving, litigation, relationship changes, surgery, etc.)

Gain Self-Confidence and Develop High Self-Worth

Acknowledge yourself as a unique, whole person. Be proud of who you are. Taking charge means creating a positive self-worth, a healthy body image, and a strong mind/body connection. Accept and love yourself, know that you are worthy and deserve the best, believe in yourself, and expect the best. Keep in mind that nobody is perfect. In fact, we are all perfectly imperfect. However, when you lack a positive self-image or self-worth, you invariably overreact and make the wrong choices or decisions in your life.

Visualize yourself as a winner. See yourself winning at the game of life. Take stock of your most positive features or characteristics. Write a paragraph summarizing your ten most positive qualities. Ask an intimate friend or loved one to do the same. Make the commitment to believe in yourself. Ask yourself, what will it take to see yourself as a winner? What will it take to believe in yourself? Now then, go for it! Remember, life is what you make of it. Life is always happening. Are you?

Utilize Dynamic Willpower and Self-Determination to Create the Habits of Success

Your willpower gives you the authority to control the direction of your life. Your willpower makes something out of nothing and makes the impossible possible. With willpower, you can make choices, set goals, and take deliberate actions to achieve these goals despite opposition, difficulty, or adversity. Strengthening your willpower gives you the focus to carry out the highest intentions of your thinking. Where there is a will, there is a way to get the job done well.

Dynamic willpower has an electric charge that energizes your physical and mental body. It is a necessary link between your mind and the performance of your body. Your willpower gives you the vision to enrich the quality of your life. Take the initiative. Your willpower is the power of your mind to purposefully control your actions. Utilize your willpower to develop the habit of success. Concentrating your will creates favorable results. Affirmations (statements that reflect strong positive convictions, beliefs, and feelings) can be used to develop and strengthen your willpower.

Use these affirmations to take charge of your life for whatever situations you want to create (i.e., happiness, wellness, success, etc.)

I need to be _____ , _____ ,

_____

I want to be _____ , _____ ,

_____

I deserve to be _____ , _____ ,

_____

I will be _____ , _____ ,

_____

I am _____ , _____ ,

_____

Practice these affirmations frequently throughout the day, especially in the early morning and before you go to bed at night.

Your willpower is revealed through your self-determination. Self-determination gives you the power to take charge of your life. This means you are willing to stand up for what you believe and take the necessary risks for your beliefs, even in the face of adversity. Squarely face up to the three greatest obstacles or conflicts in your life. Take a stand on the major issues at home or at work. Visualize what you see as optimal in your life, then will it your way. Be opportunistic, and go for it with confidence. Have the grit and guts to stand up for what you believe.

Make the Appropriate Adjustments to Stay in Charge of Your Life

Taking charge of your life means taking responsibility for modifying your behavior. It means making adjustments to changes so that you can stay happy, prosperous, and fulfilled. Remember, the one constant in life is change, and you will need to be resourceful to stay in command.

Imagine that you are a sailor in the boat of life. Your goal is to reach a faraway island. The winds are bound to change. Do not be angry and fight the changing winds. You have the ability to make adjustments by trimming the sails to get to where you want to go. Take charge of your lifeboat, and you will arrive at your desired destination.

Taking charge means being adaptable, especially in the face of adversity. It means making the best out of your circumstances.

What can you do to become more open-minded and flexible?

What adjustment must you make at work or at home to effectively take charge of your life regardless of what is happening around you?

Be Proud of Who You Are

Taking pride in yourself and your values is the key strategy in upholding strong positive belief systems. You are a unique individual, and it is very important to focus on your self-respect.

Describe the ten best human qualities you have. Ask a loved one to share with you what your ten strongest attributes are.

What action steps will it take to believe in yourself?

What changes in your personality do you need to make to fully accept yourself?

Acquire the Mechanics of Self-Care

Taking charge of your life is about getting your papers in order and keeping them in order so you can thrive at any age. *To fully realize your visions, you will need to stay vital, potent, enthusiastic, and fit.* In other words, wellness is a prerequisite to reaching and sustaining your dreams. This is especially important when you are in pursuit of a complete and balanced lifestyle.

Surely you have figured out by now that you will need a strong body, clear mind, loving heart, and courageous spirit to stay in charge and enjoy it. You will need meaning and purpose in your life. You probably also realize that learning how to cherish and nourish a deep soul mate relationship will inspire and enrich your path.

Taking responsibility for your life is only the beginning. You must follow through with the appropriate actions to nourish your whole being. Accepting self-responsibility without initiating appropriate self-nurturing activities is akin to bringing the wood to the fireplace but not starting the fire!

The mechanics of self-care teach you how to take charge of your life. Self-care means a daily consistent devotion to a physical fitness program. It also means having regular eating habits and eating high quality, nutritious, superior foods. In addition, it also means to develop your natural inherent healing powers through a commitment to daily meditation and prayer. Self-nurturing means cultivating equanimity and peace of mind. It means finding time each day to enjoy yourself and have fun within the structure of your responsibilities and chores. Self-care also means that you make the time for nurturing and rewarding your relationships. Do not get trapped in using the excuse that you do not have enough time in the day to care for yourself. You can easily waste at least that much time in idle nothingness, boredom, watching TV, reading sensational magazines or newspapers, taking unnecessary naps, or indulging in unnecessary sleep. What about the amount of energy you lose when you are emotionally distracted, depressed, or feeling emotional distress? In other words, taking charge of your life means that you care enough about yourself that you will respect, love, nurture, and reward yourself daily. The truth is that unless you take charge and create a high performance lifestyle, your lifestyle will take charge of you.

Remember, you are what you choose to think, feel, and do. The choice is yours. Exercise your powerful option to come alive and take charge of the way you live. Embrace the total and full responsibility for your choices. Make the determined commitment to be rich in life. Selectively gain control of your emotional life. Choose positive emotions over negative ones. Take charge of your thinking. Choose positive thoughts over negative ones. Create the vision of your optimal lifestyle. Organize a responsible plan of action to realize these dreams. Fortify your actions with positive personal belief systems. Marry the responsibility to take charge of your life. Be sure to have fun in the process! Make the necessary changes in your life. Take the necessary risks. Be true to yourself. It is your life. Stand up and be counted. You can get what you want. Come alive to who you are, and take charge of your life.

4
Acquire the Habit of Happiness

THIS CHAPTER will broaden your horizons and teach you the secrets to lasting happiness. Anywhere you travel, any place you choose to go, all cultures have one language in common. People everywhere want to be happy. Happiness is the emotional key to wellness. In the simplest of terms, it makes your life worth living. The fact is that happiness and love heal your heart.

A happy face, a happy smile, a happy laugh is happiness. While it is working for you, it does you the favor of slowing down your aging process. Happiness is heartfelt inner joy. Healing your heart goes deep into your soul. When you are happy inside, your heart comes alive. "Acquire the Habit of Happiness" is the fourth rule for High Performance Living and is the emotional corner-stone of preventive medicine. It teaches you to come to your own emotional rescue and become your own hero or heroine.

Thomas Jefferson, one of the founding fathers of this great country, had it straight when he wanted every American to have the right to life, liberty, and the pursuit of happiness. Happiness invigorates, inspires, and energizes your life. Similarly, depression, anxiety, and unhappiness drain your life. Emotional self-abuse and emotional mediocrity drain your lifestyle. You will have to jump some challenging hurdles on the path to lasting happiness.

Happiness keeps you in touch with the lighter side of life. When you are happy, you feel special and excited to be alive. True happiness is a bright, shining candle that brightens up your life. In fact, when you are happy, you have things to look forward to all day long, from work to passion and romance.

When you are in sync with your beliefs and principles and at the same time are in harmony with your emotions, happiness becomes the story of your life. To develop the habit, you will need to become familiar with your feelings and emotions. It is common to feel emotional; your emotions are the expression of your feelings. The movement of your feelings through your mind, body, and soul is the essence of your emotional life. Your emotions of love, joy, and excitement are the creative principles that make your life priceless! When you are in love, your heart is warm, turned on, and tuned in to your deepest emotions. Joy inspires you, and excitement stimulates you. Fear, anger, hurt, disappointment, and frustration are some negative emotions that can keep you from feeling well.

Happiness is the manifestation of your love relationship with life. It takes your breath away. It empowers you to fill up each day with loving and healing energy to enrich the lives of others and yourself. Rich in love, you are a winner!

The purpose of this chapter is to encourage you to make happiness a way of life. Positive emotions are necessary for the optimal function of your mind, body, and soul. In fact, your thoughts, behavior, and personality are emotionally conditioned. Without happiness, life can become a burdensome treadmill of overload, effort, and disappointment.

Frank Found Out

Frank would never have believed that his life would take a turn toward emotional bankruptcy. He was bright, clever, and able. Frank was voted most likely to succeed by his graduating class at business college. Frank's friends remember him saying that he was going to be a successful millionaire.

Sure enough, within four years after graduating, Frank had started a landslide of financial successes. His Madison Avenue wheelings and dealings were to provide security for him and his family for the rest of his life. But, what price glory? Frank worked twelve to fifteen hours a day and found himself taking home projects and assignments on the weekends. When Frank was jogging, he would be thinking about business deals. When he was playing racquetball, he would be timing his investments in the stock market. In fact, when he was in the bedroom, he was still thinking about the boardroom. Frank began to lose his own natural feelings. He did not hear the birds singing, and he had become a success at being a fast-paced, high-powered business executive.

One sunny Saturday afternoon, Frank took his sailboat out for a cruise. The winds were blowing strong from the North. There were small craft warnings, but Frank ignored them. Two hours later, he would go through the most horrifying experience of his life.

Some of Frank's fishing gear was mechanically loose, he lost control of the boat, it crashed against the rocks, and the gear came down on him and crushed him. He screamed for his life. A neighbor's little boy saw the boat crash in the harbor, and his mother called the ambulance. Luckily for Frank, a few minutes later, he was in a downtown emergency room getting mouth to mouth resuscitation.

Frank then went through eight hours of emergency surgery. A team of seven surgeons saved his life. Frank left the operating room alive, but one of his kidneys, one of his lungs, one of his testicles, his spleen, 50 percent of his liver, and three feet of colon were left in the pathology lab. They were removed due to profuse hemorrhaging.

Frank recovered from the surgery during the next six months to a year. His insurance policy left him a disabled multi-millionaire. Frank finally had his money. His remarks moved me when I saw him at my tenth college reunion, "Barnet, once, I thought I'd give anything to be rich, and I have. Now I would give everything I have to have my missing parts back and be whole again. All you need in life is to be healthy and happy...nothing more, nothing less!" Frank learned the most important lesson of his life the hard way. Frank was very capable of making corporate decisions that were technical and complicated. Unfortunately, Frank's work life had gotten him so imbalanced that he needed a tragedy to get in touch with his feelings.

When order replaces disorder and serenity replaces chaos, you know the habit of happiness is working. You see, this important habit teaches you to make the best of your life and to make light of your troubles. It guides you to create a favorable emotional response to the changes in your life. It encourages you to find the good in any and all circumstances.

Furthermore, the habit of happiness teaches you how to stay in touch with your feelings, both good and bad. Disappointments, emotional disturbances, and emotional upheavals are a very real part of life. Few of us have had any skilled emotional guidance or emotional mentors, so we are usually not prepared for emotional upheaval. Negative feelings can interfere with how you function, think, and make decisions. In fact, when bad feelings arise, they trigger an internal radar telling you that

RULE #4: ACQUIRE THE HABIT OF HAPPINESS   71

something is not right. This is called anxiety. It is telling you that one of your emotional needs is being threatened or that something is missing in your life.

The habit of happiness gives you the greatest gift in your life; emotional fulfillment. Emotional fulfillment is achieved when you actively satisfy your most fundamental emotional needs. You need to love and be loved. You need to be needed and need to feel love for others, for a higher purpose, and the whole of creation. You need to feel appreciated, acknowledged, valued, and cared about. In primary love relationships, you need to feel cherished and respected. You also have an intuitive need for fulfilling relationships and connecting with the spirit of others. You have a driving need to belong, a wholesome need to be yourself, and a need to effectively relate to the opposite sex. As usual, it is all up to you. Emotional fulfillment is the art of acquiring the habit of happiness.

The habit of happiness will prevent you from being unhappy. Positive loving feelings nourish your whole being; heart, mind, body, and soul. The habit of happiness keeps your focus on emotional wellness. When you are not in tune with your real feelings, it is common to become fixated on work or obsessed with alcohol, drugs, money, sex, gambling, or codependent relationships. The habit also teaches you to turn your conflicts into opportunities and triumphs, and in so doing, create your own emotional fulfillment.

In fact, you own the habit when you learn how to acknowledge your positive feelings and at the same time, read your negative feelings and validate them as being real. The habit gives you the strength to experience unpleasant feelings as a breakthrough into new levels of emotional sensitivity.

In fact, fear, emotional pain, frustration, disappointment, and anxieties are primary feelings. When you suppress them, you begin to lose touch with yourself. All too often, this is due to being overly busy, caught up in your own narcissistic thinking, or obsessed with common addictions of our society (food, work, alcoholism, TV, etc.).

Emotional self-awareness is key. When you deny, suppress, or lose touch with your primary feelings of fear, pain, frustration, hurt, and disappointment, secondary feelings of anger, resentment, and worry start to accumulate. Repressed emotions throw you out of balance, build up stress, and drain your immune system.

The habit of happiness guides you to stay in touch with any negative feelings as they arise and not hide them for days to weeks to years. It teaches you to find a way to constructively express how you feel about being hurt, frightened, and rejected and keeps your emotional life up to date. This is called meaningful communication—learning how to express yourself, not only when things are going well but also when things are not going well. When you have a quarrel with your lover or disagree about how you do things, learn to express how you feel, ask for what you need, work things out with respect, and keep your relationship fresh and in the moment. A misunderstanding with a good friend needs to be openly discussed. When you feel taken advantage of at work or you do not like your job, get in touch with what it will take to do a better job and tell your employer what you believe will make your work more meaningful. Without these communication skills, you usually walk through life in the silent majority of the emotionally wounded. Unresolved emotional wounds create fears and negative belief systems. In time, this can destroy the quality of your life.

Carve Out Your Personal Magnetism

The habit of happiness creates High Performance Living because the happiness habit works like a loving emotional magnet.

It attracts value, joy, and happiness into your life. Positive emotions attract love and magnetize positive energy. Negative emotions repel love and attract negative energy. You can tell you have the habit when there is an abundance of love and joy around you. You know you can improve your habit when you can have more love and joy in your life.

Emotional Consistency Is the Key

The bottom line in making happiness a reality comes from sound, consistent emotional living. Having the courage to live up to your deepest heartfelt emotional convictions day in and day out is the essence of emotional consistency. To be accurately diagnosed with owning the habit of happiness means you are consistently happy. This takes into consideration having a positive emotional reaction to whatever comes up or goes down around you. Emotional consistency is driven by your daily commitment to yourself to be healthy and happy. Do you make the effort? Have you made that commitment?

When you begin to walk the path of emotional consistency, you invite the warrior of emotional self-reliance to join you. Emotional self-reliance is born out of your own personal, insatiable appetite for life. It is a never say die attitude. Emotional self-sufficiency teaches you to take the full responsibility to see that your emotional needs are consistently met. This is why you must develop your emotional skills, so in the long run, you can experience emotional fulfillment.

The consistency of your emotional self-confidence keeps the pieces of your emotional puzzle connected. The truth is that as part of everyday living, unexpected things happen. It is not unusual that something could bother or upset you.

Disappointments come and go. You need to have the confidence to act appropriately and keep your emotional life in balance.

Consistent happiness is a skill. Being a great person requires the same level of skill as being a great surgeon! Imagine learning surgery without a mentor, a teacher, or a professor. Cutting out healthy tissue or making wrongful incisions would eventually teach you by trial and error, but why pay the price?

Happiness skills teach you to create a positive inner lifestyle no matter what is happening in your life on the outside. Happy people retain their sense of humor and have a natural way of being lighthearted and fun-loving. Happy people act with the greatest of ease to reach the goals or objectives they have in mind. Why? Because happy people know the meaning of love...love for life, love for loved ones, love for spirit, love for the universe, love for God, love for themselves! The good news is that emotional consistency is within your reach. All you will have to do is practice the exercises and the action steps that are explained at the end of this chapter.

Emotional Self-Assessment

To become emotionally consistent, you must know your true feelings and not run away from them. Are you so busy with what is going on around you that you are unaware of emotional experiences you feel each day? Are you in touch with your own level of happiness? Is there room for more happiness in your life?

Emotional self-awareness calls for an honest declaration of underlying feelings. By taking inventory of how you feel during the course of the day, you can find out whether you are operating from a position of loving strength or stressful mood fluctuations. To help you get acquainted with the spectrum of what you feel, consider what percentage of a typical day you spend feeling the following emotions.

_____happy	_____bored	_____joyful
_____annoyed	_____relaxed	_____irritated
_____content	_____vengeful	_____comfortable
_____anxious	_____sexy	_____deprived
_____needy	_____lonely	_____frightened
_____angry	_____loving	_____passionate
_____hurt	_____alert	_____enthusiastic
_____sad	_____bitter	_____grief-stricken
_____cheerful	_____excited	_____supportive
_____vibrant	_____needed	_____resentful
_____rejected	_____insecure	_____depressed

It will not take long to figure out that you feel happiest when you feel loved, nourished, and supported. When you get stuck and are not sure what you are feeling, close your eyes, empty your mind, and realize that the universal spirit loves you. Take some deep breaths, give yourself a few moments to get in touch, and then ask yourself what you really feel (not what you think). Be patient until you break through and get to your real feelings.

Another way to become an expert with what you are feeling is to keep track of your emotions, on the hour, using the main feeling categories on the following page as guidelines. Within a few days, with a little support from your friends and loved ones, you will get good at it. Otherwise, you can get so wrapped up with survival, chores, and details, you become a victim of your own emotionally constipated lifestyle. Remember, feelings are not what we think about how we feel. For example, "I think I'm happy, I seem to be excited, or I believe I'm angry." Feelings are felt from the heart, such as "I feel happy, I feel excited, or I feel embarrassed."

Heartfelt Communication to Enrich Your E.Q. (Emotional Quotient)

Glad	Sad	Mad
happy	lonely	angry
excited	heavy	aggravated
hopeful	troubled	exasperated
joyful	helpless	irritated
satisfied	gloomy	agitated
delighted	grief	furious
encouraged	overwhelmed	enraged
grateful	distant	infuriated
confident	despondent	hostile
inspired	discouraged	bitter
relieved	distressed	pessimistic
touched	dismayed	resentful
proud	disheartened	disgusted

Tired	Scared	Confused
exhausted	afraid	frustrated
fatigued	fearful	perplexed
inert	terrified	hesitant
lethargic	startled	troubled
indifferent	nervous	uncomfortable
listless	panicky	torn
weary	jittery	withdrawn
overwhelmed	horrified	apathetic
fidgety	anxious	embarrassed
helpless	worried	hurt
heavy	anguished	uneasy
sleepy	lonely	irritated

Peaceful	Loving	Playful
tranquil	warm	energetic
calm	affectionate	effervescent
content	tender	invigorated
engrossed	appreciative	zestful
absorbed	friendly	refreshed
expansive	sensitive	stimulated
serene	compassionate	impish
loving	grateful	alive
blissful	nurtured	exuberant
satisfied	amorous	giddy
relaxed	trusting	adventurous

Now that you are getting a feeling for the spectrum of emotional self-awareness, take a good look at the feelings that are likely to be present when your needs are being met.

absorbed	contented	exuberant	interested	rapturous
adventurous	cool	fascinated	intrigued	refreshed
affection	curious	free	invigorate	relieved
alert	dazzled	friendly	involved	satisfied
alive	delighted	fulfilled	joyful	secure
amazed	eager	gay	jubilant	sensitive
appreciation	ecstatic	glad	keyed-up	spellbound
aroused	effervescent	gleeful	loving	splendid
astonished	elated	glorious	mellow	stimulated
blissful	electrified	glowing	merry	surprised
breathless	encouraged	good-humored	mirthful	tenderness
buoyant	energetic	grateful	moved	thankful
calm	engrossed	gratification	optimism	thrilled
carefree	enjoyment	groovy	overwhelmed	touched
cheerful	enlivened	happy	overjoyed	tranquil
comfortable	enthusiastic	helpful	peaceful	trust
complacent	exalted	hopeful	pleasant	warm
composed	exhilarated	inquisitive	proud	wide-awake
concerned	expansive	inspired	quiet	wonderful
confident	expectant	intense	radiant	zestful

Furthermore, the following feelings are likely to be present when your needs are not being satisfied. Only you really know the truth about how you feel.

afraid	despair	frightened	keyed-up	shaky
aggravated	despondent	frustrated	lassitude	shocked
agitation	detached	furious	lazy	skeptical
alarm	disappointed	gloomy	let-down	sleepy
aloof	discouraged	grief	lethargy	sorrowful
angry	disgruntled	guilty	listless	sorry
anguish	disgusted	hate	lonely	spiritless
animosity	disheartened	heavy	mad	startled
annoyance	disinterested	helpless	mean	surprised
anxious	dislike	hesitant	melancholy	suspicion
apathetic	dismayed	horrified	miserable	terrified
apprehensive	displeased	horrible	mopey	thwarted
aroused	disquieted	hostile	nervous	tired

aversion	distressed	hot	nettled	troubled
bad	disturbed	hurt	overwhelmed	uncomfortable
bitter	downcast	impatient	passive	unconcerned
blah	downhearted	indifferent	perplexed	uneasy
bored	dread	inert	pessimistic	unglued
breathless	dull	infuriated	provoked	unhappy
brokenhearted	edgy	inquisitive	puzzled	unnerved
chagrined	embarrassed	insecure	rancorous	unsteady
cold	embittered	insensitive	reluctance	upset
concerned	exasperated	intense	repelled	uptight
confused	exhausted	irate	resentful	vexed
cool	fatigued	irked	restless	weary
cross	fearful	irritated	sad	withdrawn
credulous	fidgety	jealous	scared	woeful
depressed	forlorn	jittery	sensitive	worried

Action Steps

It is now time to learn how to acquire the habit of happiness. You have the necessary power of spirit to be happy.

Make the Commitment

The commitment to being emotionally consistent is born out of a commitment to yourself to be happy and whole. It begins with understanding your need to experience your ultimate emotional fulfillment so your life can realize its full potential.

It calls for the commitment and desire to be happy, healthy, and free. How much bliss time do you have every day to appreciate and love your life? To be sure you have enough, you will need seven emotional tools. These seven emotional convictions lead to emotional consistency and build the habit of happiness.

Emotional rebound. Spring right back from a disappointment. You can convert your emotional setbacks into opportunities for personal growth and development. Expect adversity because it will be there. We all grow and get tougher with adversity. Regardless of what happens, use the momentum of disappointments to spring you forward to improve the quality of life, your business, and relationships with family and loved ones. When disappointment comes, one step back is followed by two steps forward. This is what emotional rebounding is all about.

Emotional pursuit. Pursue the process of happiness. This is called emotional pursuit. The fact is you become good at what you become interested in and spend your time doing. Get to understand yourself, and take an interest in being happy. Take an interest in becoming a good tennis player, parent, pianist, or husband, and eventually, you will get good at it.

Find out what the most interesting things in your life are. What is it that you are attracted to more than anything else? When you pursue your natural interests, you become happier. Spend your time doing what you love to do, and watch your emotions creatively and spontaneously express themselves. Take charge of your life, and go after what turns you on. This is emotional pursuit. Reach out for love and wisdom. Give your emotional life a chance to find spontaneous expression. Go forward.

Emotional perseverance. Happiness is everywhere, but you have to look for it. You can only find what you are looking for. If you are not looking for it, you will not find it. I remember from medical school, when you do not look for an enlarged heart, you will not find it. When you do not look for a new job, it usually does not come knocking on your door. It is not common to meet new people in your backyard.

Emotional perseverance calls for the kind of endurance that turns all endeavors into positive, favorable emotional experiences. Conditions arise in your life to challenge you to become a stronger more complete person. Emotional perseverance teaches you to build faith and keep the faith to maintain the happiness.

Remember, perseverance furthers. Be persistent. You will get good at what you practice. There will always be difficulties and setbacks. Utilize these moments every day to fortify your resolve. Make sure being happy is a main goal in your life. Be patient with yourself. Emotional perseverance will breed the habit of happiness.

Expect to find joy and seek fulfillment in every experience. From the depths of your self-confidence, consistently create positive new emotional experiences. Perseverance furthers emotional fulfillment.

Emotional magnetism. When you are happy, vibrant, and enthusiastic, good things will come to you. Focus on your heart, and radiate pure love and joy. Allow nothing to interfere with your most positive loving vibrations. Send your healing loving vibrations to all your loved ones, and feel the love for your loved ones every day.

Feel love for life on a consistent daily basis in the morning when you awake and at night before you sleep. Send your love and joy unconditionally to the spirit and the universe.

To become an effective emotional magnet, practice this meditation for at least five to ten minutes a day. Send love and joy to your loved ones for at least five minutes, then spend another five minutes receiving love and joy back into your heart. In other words, radiate love and joy, then magnetize love and joy. This will empower your emotional magnet, because your love and joy attracts more love and joy. Then love, in the form of affection and acknowledgment, can be attracted to you. In time, your emotional magnet will carve out a lifestyle of favorable expansive heartfelt experiences. Similarly, if you are negative and unhappy, your negative emotional magnet will attract more and more negative things in your life. Radiate happiness, and happiness will come back to you.

Emotional self-reliance. Put your hands on the wheel, and take charge of your emotional life. It is your full responsibility to see to it that your emotional needs are met. Emotional self-reliance means you are the only one who can create happiness for yourself. Other people can be supportive and inspiring, but they cannot provide the happiness for you.

Happiness does not come from "when-itis" or "if only," as if outside circumstances can fulfill you. Happiness comes from within. Be strong, warm, sensitive, and vulnerable. Be compassionate and understanding. Forgive yourself for being perfectly imperfect.

When fervor and passion move you, take your inner stand. Allow your excitement to feel romantic emotionalism. When you feel and experience the ring of truth, follow it. Your inner voice wants you to be happy. Learn to trust your own feelings. Whatever it takes to make you happy will enable you to make the appropriate adjustments and give direction to your emotional life. Becoming emotionally self-reliant breeds emotional consistency and sound emotional judgment. In time, emotional self-reliance makes you emotionally independent to feel for yourself and act accordingly.

Emotional support. Emotional support means you create resourceful intrapersonal and interpersonal emotional support systems. Be emotionally supportive to loved ones and people in your life. Create lasting friendships. Learn to listen and be a good friend. Give and share with others. Create a diversified emotional support system between friends, loved ones, hobbies, and interests. This will enrich your happiness.

Also, recruit your intrapersonal (within yourself) support systems. Specialize in being your own best friend. Nurture and understand yourself. Stand by your convictions, and stand up for what you believe. Be true to yourself. Get in touch with who you are and what you love to do. Not only share it, but make it happen and recruit the proper support. When you have fallen in love with love itself and have diversified hobbies and recreational activities, you will know what it means to have emotional support in your life. To further your emotional consistency, practice the following meditation for five to ten minutes twice a day. Close your eyes, breathe deeply, and picture everything you touch become richer in happiness and love. See everyone you come in contact with healthier and happier.

Emotional balance. The habit of happiness teaches you to become an emotionally balanced person. By keeping in touch with the love in your heart and appreciating the positive things and blessings in your life, no matter what you are going through, you will be able to stay centered and grounded. Staying young at heart will keep you youthful and balanced. Search for personal freedom, and commit to lasting happiness. This will help you find your balance.

When you are emotionally balanced, you live each moment in life to its fullest. You can appreciate yourself, as well as the magnificence of life, and see the beauty in others. When you are in balance, you can keep in touch with the love in your heart, no matter what you are going through.

Go deep into the hidden chambers of your soul, and balance out your emotions. Use the light in your soul and the love in your heart to face any emotional darkness that can surface. Acknowledge the beauty around you, and appreciate the love within you. This will balance out your emotions.

Size Up Your Emotional Consistency

Please review and score from 1–5, 5 being the strongest, how well you fare with these seven emotional skills.

	Strong		Average		Weak
Emotional Rebound	5	4	3	2	1
Emotional Pursuit	5	4	3	2	1
Emotional Perseverance	5	4	3	2	1
Emotional Magnetism	5	4	3	2	1
Emotional Self-Reliance	5	4	3	2	1
Emotional Support	5	4	3	2	1
Emotional Balance	5	4	3	2	1

Total Points: _____

28–35   Strong sense of well-being and able to keep emotionally consistent. You've got the habit!

21–27   Happiness is incomplete and can escape you. Concentrate on making a little more effort at emotional consistency, regardless of your situation.

7–20   Weakened sense of inner joy. Need to focus more on getting in touch with your feelings and having more fun. Keep it lighter at all levels.

When I was a little boy, there was one thing that meant more to me than anything else in the whole wide world...when I felt great, I felt alive. Then, I knew everything was alright. Now, I am not a little boy anymore, but I still feel the same way.

Take the fourth rule of High Performance Living to the limit. Just commit to being happy, and discover what makes you happy. Have fun everyday, and remember your sense of humor. Create lasting friendships, share, and be close to your loved ones. Keep it simple, keep it light, keep it balanced, and enrich other people's lives. The habit of happiness will not let you down.

You see, the habit of happiness enables you to pinpoint troubled spots in your life. The habit of happiness teaches you to create high performance and enduring productivity in the context of being happy. When you lose touch with your heartfelt emotions, the habit of happiness will prevent you from becoming fixated on work or obsessed with alcohol, drugs, money, or sex. The habit of happiness will prevent you from being unhappy. Happiness gives you the clarity to focus on wellness and prioritize the most important things in your life. Then you can sort out the wheat from the chaff. The habit also teaches you to turn your conflicts into opportunities and triumphs and, in so doing, create your own emotional fulfillment.

Now, then, in one-hundred words or less, describe in detail what really makes you happy. Then determine what action steps you can take to heal your heart and own the habit of happiness.

5

Cleanse Your Body Regularly

NUTRITIONAL CLEANSING is a time-honored form of natural healing dating from biblical times to the sweat lodges of Native Americans. The idea is to clear out your system. Cleansing is a powerful, self-regulating nutritional tool. The focus is to purify your organs and your bodily fluids. "Cleanse Your Body Regularly" is the fifth rule of High Performance Living. Its purpose is to strengthen your immune system, rejuvenate your metabolism, and release toxins from the body.

What gets in the body that requires you to cleanse? The body builds up metabolic toxins and waste daily. Nutritional cleansing authentically solves the modern-day dilemma of how to rid the body of environmental, nutritional, and emotional toxins that are retained at a cellular level. Nutritional poisons accumulate from overconsuming artificial chemicals, preservatives, fats, processed sugars, salt, animal protein, and fast foods. Environmental toxins build up from air pollution, smog, traffic, pesticides, high density living, contamination of the water supply, and from substance abuse. Emotional toxins that need to be cleansed arise from stress, anxiety, and self-abuse.

What happens if you do not cleanse your body of these toxins? An overload of poisons in your system increases the risk of disease and accelerated aging. Excess toxins cause structural damage to the cells in your body. Damage to the structure of tissues leads to organ dysfunction. This increases your vulnerability to burnout and degenerative illness.

Acid poisons accumulate from eating processed sweets, starches, nutritionally empty junk food, meat, chicken, pork, and dairy products, and mercury-laden seafood. Over-acidity causes corrosion as an early sign of impending degenerative toxemia. One of the main objectives of the cleansing diet is to aid the kidneys in establishing the proper alkaline-acid balance of your over-acidified bodily fluids. Cleansing your bloodstream, liver, spleen, and lymphatic system clears out the debris, grease, and grime that are circulating through your glands and tissues. In the process of cleansing, poisons lodged in the vital organs and fat deposits are loosened up. The dead weight of devitalized toxins in bones, muscles, and joints are washed out. Your circulation gets the chance to fight off its internal garbage. In effect, the cleansing diet literally lightens up your metabolism.

What are the right foods to eat to cleanse your body? The essence of nutritional cleansing is to eat predominantly fresh living, uncooked, pure foods such as fresh fruits, raw vegetables, and fresh squeezed fruit and vegetable juices. I call this a high enzyme, high alkaline, raw food diet. Organic foods are preferred. These are foods that have been grown without the use of artificial chemicals and pesticides. However, when organic produce is not available, choose high quality fresh food, and make sure that all food is cleaned well.

What Might You Eat on a Typical Day of Cleansing?

Breakfast	Fresh squeezed fruit juices or smoothies Fruits and almonds
Lunch	Leafy green fresh vegetable salad with sun-flower seeds and herbal dressing *or* Veggie taco with raw vegetables rolled into a corn tortilla with natural salsa
Dinner	Carrot-celery-beet juice Fresh, mixed vegetable salad with seasoned herbal dressing Steamed vegetable platter or mixed vegetable soup or baked potato or baked yam.

Keep in mind that cleansing is a step toward better health and not a matter of deprivation. Cleansing will give you energy and leave you feeling fresh and light. The attitude you take toward the cleansing diet as toward any meal is critical. It is of the utmost importance that you:

- Enjoy your foods and the environment you eat them in (not a cold taco in the car).
- Look at each complete meal as a step toward performing better.
- Acknowledge the time and money saving wisdom in cleansing. Cleansing foods are less expensive than pre-packaged, processed foods. You can grow your own sprouts. Buying and preparing the food in advance leaves you more time to enjoy other things.

Who needs to cleanse? Everyone who has the desire to lead a healthy and disease free life will benefit from cleansing. In fact, everybody has the need to cleanse their body, and it is recommended for people eighteen years of age or older. In fact, I have often been quoted as saying that "unless you make time for cleansing, you have to make time for illness." Cleansing is good, sound, nutritional common sense. It is certainly necessary for quality autos and high-tech machinery to require regular servicing and upkeep to maintain their same efficient performance as when they were new. Why not do the same for your mind and body? Everyone experiences wear and tear in our high stressed world. Remember, the more toxic the environment, the more stress you have, and the more artificial the food you eat, the greater your need for nutritional cleansing.

How often should you cleanse? Cleansing is recommended for one day every week and for five consecutive days every three months. Weekly cleansing prevents the build up of unnecessary poisons. It keeps your bodily fluids up to date. This washes out any toxins from abuse or overload during the week.

Seasonal Timing Counts

Seasonal cleansing every three months, done quarterly (at each equinox) simplifies your life. The fundamental principle is that you need to get in a rhythm with yourself, your environment, and the cycles of nature. Nature is always changing and so are you. Your March cleansing prepares you for spring. Your June cleansing gets you ready for summer. The winter cleansing wards off the impending holiday flu.

To be well and stay that way, you have to keep in balance with the inevitable cyclical changes in the climate and weather. A great deal of your health has to do with keeping abreast of the natural changes taking place as the seasons change. When you do it right, it is called being in tune with nature.

Optimal health is actually the ability to stay well in spite of the inevitable cyclical changes in weather and life events. Have you ever noticed how most everyone at work or school is coming down with a virus at the very time there is a change in the season? That is where the term "under the weather" originates. It is the responsibility of your cleansing program to sustain inner strength and balance so you are not thrown off course. Who can afford the loss of time from work or play?

The Rhythm Method of the Cleansing Program

The rhyme and reason of the cleansing program is to keep you in balance with the seasonal changes in your environment. To do this, the program is a quarterly plan based on the four seasons. The prescription of the cleansing program is as follows:

For Each Season

Practice five days on the cleansing program. It is best to begin ten days before each seasonal change (at the equinox or solstice). This orderly seasonal tune-up strengthens your body while it recharges your spirit.

The seasonal cleansings are as follows:

Spring Cleansing:	Seven to ten days before March 20–22 Start on or before March 10
Summer Cleansing:	Seven to ten days before June 10–22 Start on or before June 10
Autumn Cleansing:	Seven to ten days before Sept. 20–22 Start on or before September 10
Winter Cleansing:	Seven to ten days before Dec. 20–22 Start on or before December 10

Rhythm Method for Your Seasonal Cleansing Program

Spring Equinox

March 20 - April 30	Maintenance program—Cleanse one day a week
May 1 - May 5	Mid-Seasonal Detoxification* program
May 6 - June 9	Maintenance program—Cleanse one day a week
June 10 - June 15	Seasonal Cleansing program
June 16 - June 19	Maintenance program

Summer Solstice

June 20 - July 3	Maintenance program—Cleanse one day a week
Aug. 1 - Aug. 5	Mid-Seasonal Detoxification* program
Aug. 6 - Aug. 9	Maintenance program—Cleanse one day a week
Aug. 10 - Sept.15	Seasonal Cleansing program
Sept. 16 - Sept. 19	Maintenance

Autumn Equinox

Sept. 20 - Oct. 31	Maintenance program—Cleanse one day a week
Nov. 1 - Nov. 5	Mid-Seasonal Detoxification* program
Nov. 6 - Dec. 9	Maintenance program—Cleanse one day a week
Dec.10 - Dec. 15	Seasonal Cleansing program
Dec. 16 - Dec. 19	Maintenance program

Winter Solstice

Dec. 20 - Jan. 31	Maintenance program—Cleanse one day a week
Feb. 1 - Feb. 5	Mid-Seasonal Detoxification* program
Feb. 6 - March 9	Maintenance program—Cleanse one day a week
March 10 - March 15	Seasonal Cleansing program
March 16 - March 19	Maintenance program

* Add grains to the cleansing program—see Types of Cleansing programs, page 103.

Side Effects of the Cleansing Diet

During the cleansing process, a variety of new and interesting experiences can take place. There are some individuals who, from start to finish, experience nothing but well-being. Then there are those who are euphoric 85 percent of the time and at other times have an intermittent attack of fatigue or fear of the unknown. Yet, there are others who are plagued with foul body odors, catarrhal elimination, toxic skin eruptions, joint discomforts, and strange tastes in their mouths.

For those who experience splitting headaches from releasing toxins, there are two natural remedies. The first is hydrotherapy, that is to immerse yourself in a natural, fresh cold water source, such as the ocean, or take a cold shower and direct the cold water to your forehead. The other solution is to go to bed and sleep it off. Acupressure or acupuncture along large intestine (LI 11) or gall bladder (GB 20) meridians can often make the headache disappear. You can also try 100 mg of vitamin B-1 every two hours until you feel better.

Bear in mind that it is not uncommon in some 15–50 percent of patients to report some weakness and fatigue at one or two points in the first four days of cleansing. Invariably, as cellular poisons are broken up and broken loose, they pour into your circulation. This commonly causes a tired, drugged feeling. Do not fret. It is temporary. To overcome this lethargic state, you simply slow down the cleansing process by adding some protein to your program. For example, add 1½ tablespoons of brewer's yeast to fresh squeezed fruit juice, or eat a couple of celery stalks with almond butter.

Most of the time, you can prevent getting tired by adhering to your sunrise exercise and meditation routine. Tuning up your body with physical exercise before each meal will also help. With the right attitude, willpower, consistent positive thinking, and enough rest, potential side effects will be minimized. Taking the proper nutritional supplements will minimize the side effects and also reduce fatigue.

Nutritional Supplements for the Cleansing Diet

Vitamin E	400 I.U. one time with your fruit (mixed tocopherols) juice fifteen minutes before breakfast
Vitamin B-1	100 mg. one time a day (at breakfast)
Vitamin B-6	100 mg. one time a day (at breakfast)
Hi-Potency B-Complex (Super B, Mega B)	one with each meal
Vitamin C	1000 mg. two times a day (at breakfast and at dinner time)
Folic Acid	400 mcg. one time a day
Vitamin B-12	1000 mcg. once a day
Brewer's Yeast	1$\frac{1}{2}$ tbsp. twice a day blended in juice and taken between meals for a pick-up

Whether you suffer with side effects or not is very individ-ualized and is determined by your metabolic efficiency. When you are in the best of health, you will experience minimal to no side effects. Those of you whose health is more fragile will be more susceptible to discomfort. It is important to work through these phases of detoxification and move on to a higher level of physiological integrity, strength of emotional character, and uni-versal consciousness. It reminds me of the runner who runs a mile and a half and feels weak and tired. With regular conditioning and getting into better shape, he can push ahead a bit, at which point, he will be able to tolerate a two mile run with great ease. The fact is that many people experience nothing but joy and light on the cleansing diet.

Risks of the Cleansing Diet

For those individuals in good health, there are essentially no risks. The main risks of the cleansing diet are for those who are malnourished, diabetic, or hypoglycemic. When you are food dependent, usually you need to build your body up first and start with the Maintenance Diet in chapter 6. Once your body is substantially reconstructed, consult with your physician and get his or her advice on starting your cleansing program.

Another important risk is for those who stay on the cleansing diet for too long. You can over-cleanse by staying on a cleansing for longer than two to three weeks. At this point, your body chemistry can become too alkaline or experience protein, calcium, or iron imbalances. As noted, five to seven days of cleansing at one time is usually sufficient.

Some individuals may have as many as three to six bowel movements a day. It is because all the fresh vegetables and fruits are beginning to purge your intestines. If you suffer with

diverticulitis or a spastic colon, consult your doctor before starting the cleansing. The most common risk is that you may find out
within the week just how unwell you really are.

Guidelines for the Traditional High Performance Living Cleansing Program

The foods recommended are:

Seasonal Fresh Fruits and Fruit Juices	yes	All fresh fruits in season. Avoid sweetened, frozen, or canned fruits. No dried fruits. The bottom line is one fresh fruit salad per day. Emphasize pink grapefruit, grapes, berries, mangos, strawberries, watermelon, cantaloupe, oranges. Seasonal fresh fruit juice twice daily.
Fresh Vegetables and Raw Vegetable Juices	yes	All fresh vegetables with an emphasis on raw leafy greens, steamed broccoli, zucchini, and string beans. Avoid white head lettuce. Carrot, carrot-celery, or carrot-celery-beet juice once a day.
Sprouts	yes	Living sprouts are essential high enzyme, living foods for cleansing. Emphasize alfalfa, bean, and sunflower seed sprouts.
Nuts	yes	Almonds are an alkaline staple to the morning cleansing program. Walnuts, cashews, and brazil nuts are acceptable along with

		almonds for your mixed nuts at lunch. Avoid salted, oiled, commercially roasted nuts. Raw or home roasted nuts are acceptable.
Nut Butters	yes	Un-hydrogenated, unsalted peanut or almond butter is highly nutritious on a crisp celery stalk. Avoid all other nut butters.
Seeds	yes	Raw or home roasted sunflower seeds and sesame seeds are the seeds of choice for cleansing. Eat your seeds with green vegetables and not fruits.
Natural Starchy Carbohydrates	yes	Baked potatoes, corn on the cob, yams, steamed or baked squash (acorn, winter, spaghetti squash) without butter, oil, or salt is a staple of the cleansing dinner.
Herbs	yes	Peppermint, Rose Hips, Lemon Grass, Hibiscus Flower are good cleansing herbs when made into herbal tea.
Beverages and Seasonings	yes	Red cayenne pepper, fresh garlic, fresh onion, apple cider vinegar, and lemon are special all-purpose cleansing condiments.
	no	Avoid coffee, soda, diet drinks, and alcohol. Avoid all sugar and salt.
Whole Grains	no	

Legumes	no
Dairy Products	no
Eggs	no
Flesh Foods	no

Now that you know what is in and what is out, take a look at the blueprint for the cleansing diet. This will walk you through your daily food choices to make cleansing work for you.

Blueprint for the Traditional High Performance Living Cleansing Program

Early morning. Fifteen to twenty minutes of aerobic exercise, deep breathing, and invigorating hydrotherapy, followed by The Cleansing Breakfast for thirty minutes.

The Cleansing Breakfast

1) Fresh fruit juice in season (6 oz.) followed by fifteen minutes of meditation. Then,
2) Fruit Salad with two to three fresh seasonal fruits (1½ cups), and 1–2 oz. almonds (approx., 15–20) Alfalfa sprouts (as many as you like)

Mid-morning. Herbal cleansing tea

Mid-day. Go outdoors, relax your mind and body, followed by The Cleansing Luncheon for thirty minutes.

The Cleansing Luncheon

Fresh carrot juice (6 oz.)

Fifteen minutes later:

Leafy-Green Chlorophyll Salad: Garden crisp vegetables
with romaine lettuce, sprouts, tomato, and three fresh,
raw, green vegetables, with your choice of herbal salad
dressing and one of the following:

> 2 tsp. sunflower or sesame seeds
> 1/2 avocado with or without salsa
> 1–2 celery sticks with 1 tbsp. almond butter
> (unsalted) per stalk

OR

Fresh fruit juice in season (6 oz.)

Fifteen minutes later:

Cleansing Fruit and Nut Salad with 2 oz. mixed nuts,
including almonds and alfalfa sprouts

Mid-afternoon. Herbal cleansing tea

Evening. The Cleansing Dinner for thirty minutes.

The Cleansing Dinner

Fresh carrot, carrot-celery, or carrot-celery-beet juice (8 oz.)
Sprouted Garden-Fresh Salad with a variety of fresh,
raw vegetables and 2 tsp. sunflower seeds
Steamed Green Vegetable Combination (a platter of
two to three steamed green vegetables) or Vegetable
Soup (1 bowl).
Natural complex carbohydrate, to be chosen from:
Baked potato, 1 medium (no butter or salt)
Corn on the cob, 1 ear (no butter or salt)
Baked yam, 1 medium
Steamed or baked squash, 1 medium

Note: Use Cleansing Chili Salsa or avocado to flavor your starches.
Omit sunflower seeds when using avocado on starches.

After dinner. Herbal cleansing tea

When the proper food ingredients on the cleansing diet are combined together on the basis of sound food combining, you will get the best results. Knowing how to combine your food is achieved by studying the basic food groupings below:

Basic Food Groupings of Traditional Nutritional Cleansing

Group 1: Fruit Salad Combinations

Fruits have seasons of peak nutritional value. Eat only the fresh fruits in season. The fruit salad of choice changes with the seasons. The mineral balance of these fruit salad combinations becomes alkaline once digested.

Spring

Tropical Fruit Salad	papaya, pineapple, banana
Spring Salad	pineapple, banana, strawberry
Cherry Supreme Salad	cherry, peach, banana
Grape Delight Salad	green, purple, and red grapes
Mango Salad	mango, pineapple, banana

Summer

Summer Melon Salad	cantaloupe, watermelon, papaya
Nectarine Peach Salad	nectarine, peach, cherries, plums
Hawaiian Fruit Salad	papaya, mango, pineapple
Tropical Fruit Salad	papaya, pineapple, banana
Apricot Salad	apricot, peach, plum, grape, cherry
Mango Peach Salad	mango, peach, banana
Berry Salad	berries, peach, apricot
Cherry Plum Salad	cherries, plum, nectarine
Summer Grape Salad	grapes, cherries, banana

Autumn

Mixed Apple Salad	Pippin, Macintosh, and Golden apples
Autumn Salad	banana, papaya, apple
Waldorf Apple Salad	apple, pear, banana
Grape Salad	green and red grapes or any apple or pear
Pear Salad	pear, papaya, banana

Winter

Tropical Fruit Salad	pineapple, papaya, banana
Winter Citrus Salad	orange, pineapple, pink grapefruit
Grapefruit Salad	pink grapefruit, orange, banana
Orange Salad	orange, pineapple, banana
Papaya Salad	papaya, orange, banana

Group 1A: Fresh Fruit Juices (Not a Concentrate)

Spring

orange juice, grapefruit juice, pineapple juice, papaya juice

Summer

watermelon juice, cantaloupe juice, papaya juice

Autumn

apple juice, pineapple juice, pear juice, orange juice

Winter

orange juice, pineapple juice, grapefruit juice

Group 2: Leafy-Green Chlorophyll Salads

Sprouted Garden-Fresh Dinner Salad	romaine lettuce, tomato, sprouts, parsley, red onion, red cabbage, carrot
Garden-Green Chlorophyll Salad	romaine lettuce, spinach, Swiss chard, parsley, sprouts, tomato, carrot
Spice-of-Life Spinach Salad	spinach leaves, romaine lettuce, sprouts, tomato, red onion, celery
Mexican Cabbage Salad	red cabbage, green cabbage, red onion or green onion, romaine lettuce, tomato
Avocado-Tomato Grande Salad	avocado, tomato, romaine lettuce, sprouts, cucumber, beet
Radiant Radish Salad	radishes, red onion, romaine lettuce, sprouts, tomato, parsley
Raw Mushroom Salad	mushrooms, romaine lettuce, sprouts, tomato, cucumber, celery
Cauliflower Salad	cauliflower, celery, mushrooms, romaine lettuce, sprouts, tomato
Garden Pea Salad	Chinese snow peas, green peas, green or red bell pepper, romaine lettuce, sprouts, tomato
Jicama-Beet Treat	jicama, beet, carrot, romaine lettuce, sprouts, tomato
Mustard Greens Salad	mustard greens, beet greens, dandelion greens, sprouts, tomato
Super Sprouts Salad	mung bean sprouts, alfalfa sprouts, sunflower seed sprouts, romaine lettuce, tomato
Cucumber-Beet Salad	cucumber, beet, red onion, romaine lettuce, sprouts, tomato
Basic Avocado Salad	avocado, beet, beet greens, red onion, romaine lettuce, sprouts, tomato

Group 2A: Fresh Vegetable Juices

carrot juice
carrot-celery-beet-cucumber juice
carrot-celery juice
carrot-celery-string bean juice
carrot-celery-beet juice
carrot-celery-parsley-beet juice

Group 3: Steamed Green Vegetable Combinations

Broccoli-Zucchini Vegetable Platter	broccoli, zucchini, string beans
Asparagus-Broccoli Medley	asparagus, broccoli, zucchini
Cauliflower Mixed Vegetable Platter	cauliflower, zucchini, broccoli
Brussels Sprout Mixed Vegetable Platter	Brussels sprouts, zucchini, green bell peppers
Green Bean Vegetable Combination	green beans, carrots, spinach or chard
Chinese Steamed Vegetable Combination	Chinese snow peas, bok choy, jicama, carrots
Steamed Carrot-Peas Vegetable Platter	green peas, carrots, broccoli
Broccoli-Mixed Greens Vegetable Soup	broccoli, zucchini, string beans, or combinations of any of the above

The Cleansing Program keeps your metabolic "machine" in efficient running order.

Tips for Feeling Tops while Cleansing

- Eat the right foods in the spirit of moderation.
- Practice prudent undereating.
- Earn your meals with hard work or physical exercise before eating.

- Completely relax when you eat.
- Enjoy your food. Keep your mental attitude positive.
- Substitute intimate conversation, good company, and laughter for overindulgence.
- Eat only when you are hungry.
- Eat exactly what is prescribed.

Golden Rules for Cleansing

Cleansing has some fundamental rules to guide you to select and combine your food properly. Follow these simple rules, and you will be rewarded mentally and physically. Here is the bottom line:

Rule 1   Select one fruit salad with at least 1 oz. almonds for breakfast.

Rule 2   Select one vegetable salad or fruit salad at lunch.

Rule 3   Select one vegetable salad at dinner.

Rule 4   Select one starchy carbohydrate at dinner.

Rule 5   Drink one glass raw vegetable juice daily.

Rule 6   Drink two glasses seasonal fruit juice daily.

Rule 7   Avoid snacking.

Rule 8   Avoid breads, grains, legumes, dairy, or flesh proteins.

Rule 9   Take at least thirty minutes a day to enjoy each meal.

Rule 10 Be certain to drink 6–8 glasses of fluid each day.

Rule 11 Between meals, drink only herbal teas. Red Zinger, Rose Hips, Lemon Grass, Hibiscus, and Peppermint are noted for their cleansing properties.

Rule 12 Season your foods with the following: garlic, red cayenne pepper, lemon juice, lime juice, apple cider vinegar, and onions.

Types of Cleansing

There are different levels of cleansing. There are traditional cleansing programs, as described and discussed, and there is the advanced raw food only cleansing. The most aggressive cleansing program is a liquid diet of juice fasting. Finally, the modified cleansing (detoxification program) adds whole grains to fresh living foods for senior citizens, pregnant women, and those with a malnourished or depressed immune system. In other words, all individuals can find their own niche and individualize their cleansing for their own specific needs and requirements.

Physiology of Traditional Nutritional Cleansing

To initiate the healing effects of this nutritional cleansing diet, it takes at least one full day of cleansing. The release of the poisons into the circulation breaks loose a new exchange process. And that is just the kind of exchange needed for nutritional cleansing; replacing the old with the new! The idea is to keep exchanging for good health. Every time you bring substantial quality into your body, something of lesser quality that you have been holding onto osmotically leaves. In this way, you gradually reorder your system and restore proper balance. Sickness leaves in exchange for health, malnourishment departs in exchange for nourishment, and you intelligently exchange negative poisons for real energy.

Patience and persistence are necessary attributes while the internal purification process takes hold. The initial few days of discomfort that may be experienced in the five day seasonal cleanse are worth diligently enduring to in order to acquire the genuine freedom from that which pollutes, impairs, and weakens you! The last days of the nutritional cleansing, the body passes into a new level of wellness, liberated from stifling toxemic obstructions. Your thinking becomes loosened and straightforward, your emotions are unmistakable and unequivocal, and your body is serene. The breakthrough can be seen in your new brightness! The nutritional arousal of your mental, physical, emotional, and spiritual purification is fundamental to activating your very own natural healing process. The effects are far-reaching. By day five, your nutritional cleansing program creates a clear heart and renews the spirit!

The Low-Protein Vegetarian Cleansing Diet

The cleansing program is a low protein, low fat, high in simple natural carbohydrates diet. It provides anywhere from 15–20 grams of complete protein, depending upon how many nuts, seeds, avocados, potatoes, and nut butters are eaten. Cleansing diets are purposely low protein.

A low protein vegetarian diet is most conducive to a general housecleaning. The cleansing conserves metabolic energy normally utilized to digest and metabolize protein. The power behind this extra energy is shunted into electrifying the auto-purification process of cleansing the liver, spleen, pancreas, kidneys, and lymph system. Remember that a cleansing diet is not intended to be a maintenance plan. For those high performance athletes who choose to cleanse, add spirulina, brewer's yeast, or soy protein to your fruit smoothies for extra protein.

Before beginning to cleanse, ask yourself these two questions to become more familiar with your eating habits.

- What do you eat too much of?
- What do you need to eat more of?

To start your cleansing, go through your cupboards and throw out all low quality, artificial, unnatural foods. Then, take action and enjoy your cleansing! Take advantage of the cleansing formulas below to enhance your results.

Dr. Meltzer's Potassium-Rich Vegetable Broth

Recommended as an adjunct to juice fasting and cleansing diets. It is also very effective for treating digestive ailments and the nausea and vomiting of intestinal flu. Drink the following vegetable broth as desired:

1 cup zucchini	1 medium carrot
1/2 cup broccoli	1 medium potato
1/2 cup string beans	1 stalk celery
1 tbsp. parsley	1 medium beet

Add the above vegetables to 4 cups boiling water and let simmer for 20 minutes. Discard vegetables and drink the broth. Season with garlic, onion, cayenne, and kelp.

Dr. Meltzer's Red Zinger Tea

This drink is effective for treating the common cold and other upper respiratory infections (ear infections, bronchitis, sinus infections, etc.) Drink two to three times a day. For severe colds, drink every two to three hours.

1 cup Red Zinger Tea
1 tsp. honey (when desired)
1/2 lemon
1 tbsp. apple cider vinegar
pinch of red cayenne pepper

Cleansing Lemon Herbal Dressing

2/3 cup lemon juice
1/2 tsp. celery seed
3 chopped scallions
1/2 tsp. paprika
1/2 cup parsley, minced
1/2 tsp. basil
1/8 tsp. oregano
Mix all ingredients in blender, chill.

Cleansing Chili Salsa

3 tomatoes
1 green pepper
1/2 tsp. oregano
1/3 tsp. red cayenne pepper
1–2 tsp. chili powder
Combine all ingredients in blender, chill.

Remember, the cleansing program is based upon the fundamental principles of preventative medicine: keep yourself balanced to stay well. In harmony with yourself, you stand the most favorable chance to keep in harmony with your changing environment. When you are well-nourished, you can stay in charge of your life. Your cleansing program gives you the adaptability to stay internally balanced with the changing forces in the world around you.

Nutritional cleansing is decisive and efficient. It balances the chemistry of your internal organs and brings them into biochemical equilibrium with your mental and physiological needs. By the time you finish five days of cleansing, your whole being comes alive! Your body has its own biological clock, ticking away either in time or out of step with sunrise, sunset, darkness, and the change of seasons. Cleansing gets you feeling your best by synchronizing your inner clock to the natural rhythms of nature. Cleanse and be well!

Coming Alive!

Inner Strength

Inner Balance

Purification

Cleansing

Maintain Nutritional Balance

THE SIXTH RULE of High Performance Living is "Maintain Nutritional Balance." The purpose of this high performance nutritional maintenance program is to balance the chemistry of your mind and body. A well-balanced, mind/body chemistry is a necessary life-support system for all individuals. Your brain chemistry is responsible for how you think and feel, and your body chemistry determines how well you function and perform. The primary focus of nutritional balance is to build and maintain a strong and sound immune system. This will fortify your body's healing power to stay well and prevent disease.

Maintenance is based on eating your way to wellness. The High Performance Living nutritional plan provides you with the fifty essential micronutrients from vitamin A to zinc for optimal human nourishment. The high performance maintenance program is a balanced, natural foods, vegetarian-based diet with the emphasis on whole foods. This maximizes your absorption and assimilation of essential life serving nutrients. The benefit of intelligent, wholesome nutrition keeps you sharp, agile, bright, and energetic. To be solid, steady, and firm is the theme of nutritional maintenance.

The nutritional maintenance diet is for everyone, including the infant, elderly, teenager, and the mature adult. It works for the businessman, housewife, pregnant mother, laborer, professional in the city, and the cowboy in the country.

Nutritional balance requires a consistent, high fiber, low fat, chemical free, whole food eating program without unnatural preservatives.

Effective nutritional balance relies on:

- A plentiful supply of rich living food (fresh fruits, vegetables, and juices).
- A high intake of complex carbohydrates (whole grain cereals, breads and pastas, potatoes and brown rice).
- A moderate level of plant and vegetable protein, high in natural quality amino acids.
- A diet rich in trace minerals and vitamins.
- A nutritional plan, high in phytonutrients (molecules and enzymes in fresh foods that energize you).
- An abundant supply of antioxidants (anti-aging, anti-cancer, anti-stress nutrients).

Enzymes, Hormones, and Nerves Can Energize Your Body

All components of wellness from fitness to mind power to will power to relaxation depend upon the strength of your neuro-endocrine system: your nervous system and your glandular metabolism (endocrine system). Your brain is home to your central nervous system and master glands where thinking, feeling, intelligence, and behavior can be transferred from one nerve ending to another. These nerves branch out and become messenger bundles. They carry impulses from your mind to your muscles to produce action. Your glands (pituitary, adrenals, thyroid, ovary, etc.) release hormones that connect your ideas and feelings with your behavior. The objective of maintenance is to efficiently reconstruct your own body's self-regulating pharmacy of enzymes and hormones. In effect, your nerves, enzymes, and hormones connect your mind to your body. Since you rely on your neuroendocrine system for performance, it is important to feed, nourish, and care for it properly. In addition to your nerves, hormones, and enzymes, your nervous system sends messages from your mind to your body, one synapse to the next through neurochemical transmitters. In fact, these neurochemical transmitters govern the internal biochemical language of your mind/body connection.

It is very important to eat well to provide wholesome, high quality, essential micronutrients, abundant in minerals, vitamins, and amino acids to construct efficiently and synthesize these vital chemical messages. The precursors of these enzymes and hormones that regulate your metabolism are found in abundance in fresh fruits and vegetables, whole grains, nuts, seeds, and fresh squeezed juices. Living foods such as fresh fruits and vegetables keep your neuroendocrine system alive because they contain the phytonutrients (living phytochemicals) that rejuvenate your nervous system as well as your glands, organs, and tissues. Review the chart on the following page to see how valuable these phytonutrients are in defending your immune system and fighting off disease.

Antioxidants Can Make the Difference

There is a strong relationship between wholesome, fresh, living foods and high antioxidant potential. Antioxidants defend your nervous system from the damage of stress, environmental pollution, self-abuse, and aging. Antioxidants are the faculty nutrients in your diet that protect your body from arthritis, cancer, and the ill effects of alcohol, caffeine, sugar, or any other drugs. Antioxidants also strengthen your circulation, enhance cellular vitality, and enrich your immune system.

Phytonutrients	Natural Sources	Therapeutic Benefits
Flavinoids	citrus, peppers, broccoli, grapes	prevent cancer-causing hormones from binding to cell surfaces
Carotenoids	parsley, carrots, cantaloupe, spinach, kale, citrus	antioxidants inhibiting free radicals
Coumarins	peppers, strawberries, carrots, pineapple, tomatoes	inactivate carcinogenic nitrosamines
Capsaicin	peppers, beets	prevent carcinogen attachment to DNA
Allylic Sulfides	garlic, onion, leeks, chives	activate anti-cancer enzymes
Sulforaphane	broccoli	activate anti-cancer enzymes
Chlorogenic Acid	carrots, peppers, pineapple	deactivate carcinogenic nitrosamines
Phenethyl Isothiocyanate	kale, leeks, spinach	anti-carcinogens
Ellagic Acid	strawberries, grapes, raspberries	anti-carcinogens
Indole Carbinol	cauliflower	inactivate cancer-causing form of estrogen

Free radicals build up in the body from eating unnatural, chemical-ridden, artificially processed and fast foods. Free radicals are the chemical toxins in your nutritional program that act as pro-oxidants (opposite of antioxidants) that accelerate and cause damage to cells, nerves, tissues, and arteries. For example, atherosclerosis, or hardening of the arteries, is a result of overeating highly saturated fat, and the chemical toxins that build up in the arterial walls. You can diagnose the side effects of having too many free radicals (pro-oxidants) and not enough antioxidants when you fatigue, tire easily, experience stiffening of the joints, or have been diagnosed with hardening of the arteries.

Your nutritional well-being can be defined by the A-to-F Ratio:

$$\frac{\text{Antioxidants}}{\text{Free Radicals}}$$

The more antioxidants in your nutritional program and the fewer free radicals in your body, the better your nutritional balance.

Look to the list below to learn which are the best foods for your body:

High Quality Fuel (high in antioxidants)	Low Quality Fuel (high in free radicals)
whole grains	butters
fresh fruits	dairy products
fresh vegetables	saturated fats
legumes and beans	high salt food
fresh-squeezed juices	highly processed food
sprouts	beef and pork protein
nuts and seeds	caffeine
	soft drinks
	junk food
	processed sweets

The Maintenance Program Works

The nutrition of the maintenance plan invigorates your body, awakens your mind, refreshes your heart, and rejuvenates your spirit. It deliberately assembles high-quality micronutrients into the proper food combinations for optimal organic cellular function. This high quality maintenance program restores your body's warehouse of vitamins, minerals, essential amino acids, and unsaturated fatty acids. The plan establishes you as a healthy, vital human being capable of illness-free living. It enables you to function at a high level of human efficiency in whatever you are doing, without getting tired or losing your concentration. It fuels your strength of character so you can bear up under any kind of emotional and physical stress.

The maintenance plan naturally fuels your whole body to keep you looking great and feeling better. It is based upon principles that cleanse and detoxify your system while also supporting your growth and development. This is accomplished by eating a variety of fresh, living, wholesome foods. The program includes fresh fruits, raw vegetables, whole grains, legumes, and complete protein to firmly restore nuclei and cell membranes.

The anatomy of the high performance maintenance program creates the framework for nutritional healing.

The Maintenance Diet has:
- a cleansing foundation
- a detoxification background
- high-quality nutritive fiber for elimination of metabolic waste
- restorative, transforming, nourishing phytonutrients
- purification powers
- regular juice fasting program

In essence, the maintenance diet keeps your metabolism precision-like and fresh. This high performance program is a cleansing diet, a detox diet, an elimination diet, a replacement diet, and a restorative diet, all rolled into one. That is why it is so effective in keeping you well. The balancing effect of this kind of maintenance diet sustains the unification of mind, body, and spirit that stands for outstanding health.

Improve Your Sex Life

The maintenance plan will invariably improve your sex life. With a greater sense of nutritional balance, you will feel and be more potent. Women, who for years have been trying to get pregnant find themselves successfully breastfeeding and bearing children while following this maintenance plan. Men who have complained of sexual ineptness find themselves attractive and virile. Women who are plagued by fatigue and have lost their desire for passionate sex are pleasantly surprised that life has not passed them by. The balancing effect that the maintenance diet has on your bodily hormones is physiologically and mentally responsible for your more active sex drive and stronger sex life.

Long-Term Goal

The long-term goal of your nutritional maintenance program is to create inner balance and inner strength. The closer you stick to this program, the easier it will be to sustain wellness and disease-free living. Take the following nutritional quiz, and see how you select the foods you eat. Sizing up your nutritional strengths and weaknesses is an important tool to improve your nutritional program. Please take a few moments and answer these questions. Give yourself 5 points for "Always," 4 points for "Usually," 3 points for "Sometimes," 2 points for "Rarely," and 1 point for "Never." Upon completion, add your total score.

Nutritional Discretionary Quotient

Food Selection

Food Selection A:

	Always	Usually	Sometimes	Rarely	Never
I consistently eat fresh high quality foods at each meal.	5	4	3	2	1
There is a well thought out consistency and continuity to my nutritional program.	5	4	3	2	1
I read the labels for ingredients before buying food items.	5	4	3	2	1
I eat at least one bowl of a fresh fruit salad every day.	5	4	3	2	1
I eat at least one plate of vegetable salad every day.	5	4	3	2	1
I am sure to combine fresh, raw, living food with complete protein* at each and every meal.	5	4	3	2	1
I can stay away from sweets and chocolates or rich creamy desserts at will.	5	4	3	2	1
I keep the fat content of my diet down to less than 15 percent.	5	4	3	2	1

	Always	Usually	Sometimes	Rarely	Never
I choose natural, high complex carbohydrate, moderate protein, and low-fat foods.	5	4	3	2	1
I drink at least one glass of fresh vegetable juice four to five times a week.	5	4	3	2	1
I drink at least one glass of fresh squeezed fruit juice every day.	5	4	3	2	1
I eat sprouts (alfalfa, mung bean, lentil, garbanzo, etc.) at least once a day.	5	4	3	2	1
I rely on my food choices rather than vitamin supplements to provide my optimal nutritional needs.	5	4	3	2	1
I eat brown rice rather than white rice and avoid white rice at Asian restaurants.	5	4	3	2	1
I eat whole grain breads and cereals not enriched breads or cereals.	5	4	3	2	1
I follow a cleansing program at least once a week.	5	4	3	2	1
I stay away from foods that I am sensitive or allergic to.	5	4	3	2	1

*Consult text and food lists on pages 132–37 to determine complete protein requirements.

Total Points—Food Selection A:

_____

Scores above 75 are suggestive of an optimal nutritional
    program.
Scores below 60 indicate the need for a nutritional wake-
    up call.

In Section B of this quiz, score 5 for "Always" and 1 for
"Never." Upon completion, add your total score.

Food Selection B:

	Always	Usually	Sometimes	Rarely	Never
I eat some canned, packaged, or frozen fruits or vegetables every day.	5	4	3	2	1
I eat white bread, white flour tortillas, processed cereals, commercialized pizzas, or at least one refined carbohydrate every day.	5	4	3	2	1
I have indigestion after meals or during the meals.	5	4	3	2	1
I eat out at restaurants that do not serve highly nutritious foods at least one to two times a week.	5	4	3	2	1
I eat bacon, sausages, frankfurters; ham, or smoked fish at least one to two times a week.	5	4	3	2	1
I drink at least one cup of coffee a day.	5	4	3	2	1

	Always	Usually	Sometimes	Rarely	Never
I eat white crackers, potato chips, salted corn chips, or salted nuts and salted pretzels frequently.	5	4	3	2	1
I eat commercialized candy, cookies, ice cream, cake, or whipped cream at least once a week.	5	4	3	2	1
I eat pasteurized butter at least two to three times a week.	5	4	3	2	1
I drink pasteurized milk at least once a week and sometimes every day.	5	4	3	2	1
I eat the following condiments regularly: iodized salt, catsup, mustard, saccharin, jams, jellies.	5	4	3	2	1
I eat shellfish at least one to two times a week.	5	4	3	2	1
I eat red meat at least one to two times a week.	5	4	3	2	1
I eat 1 tsp. of white or brown sugar at least once a day.	5	4	3	2	1
I eat fried food at least once a week.	5	4	3	2	1
I usually eat some fruit with my vegetable meals.	5	4	3	2	1
I usually have packaged cereals or eggs first thing every morning.	5	4	3	2	1
I eat meat, fish, or poultry every day.	5	4	3	2	1

	Always	Usually	Sometimes	Rarely	Never
I eat some saturated fat in the form of dairy or lard every day.	5	4	3	2	1

Total Points—Food Selection B:

_____

A score of 19 is perfect.

Scores from 20–25 are within optimal range.

Scores above 25 suggest the need for behavior modification.

Scores above 30 suggest the need for immediate change.

One of the first steps for creating nutritional wellness is making a commitment to the quality of your diet.

Nutritional common sense dictates eating high quality foods and avoiding low quality toxic fuel.

What did you learn about the way you select your foods? Self-awareness is the breakthrough that will lead to improving the quality of your nutritional program.

Awareness without action is not enough! What will it take to apply and execute what you know is best for you?

Eating Habits

Your eating habits really count. Give yourself 5 points for "Always" and 1 point for "Never." Upon completion, add your total score.

Eating Habits A:

	Always	Usually	Sometimes	Rarely	Never
Do you center yourself and make a point to slow down before each meal?	5	4	3	2	1
Are you truly relaxed in mind and body while eating?	5	4	3	2	1
Do you have a regular time each day that you eat breakfast?	5	4	3	2	1
Do you have a regular time each day that you eat lunch?	5	4	3	2	1
Do you have a regular time each day that you eat dinner?	5	4	3	2	1
Do you chew each piece of food individually, one mouthful at a time, and avoid gulping and inhaling your food?	5	4	3	2	1
Do you enjoy your meals?	5	4	3	2	1
Do you maintain your weight within 10 percent of your ideal body weight?	5	4	3	2	1
Do you take the time to appreciate the taste of each individual food?	5	4	3	2	1

	Always	Usually	Sometimes	Rarely	Never
Do you avoid snacks between meals?	5	4	3	2	1
Do you avoid "raiding" the refrigerator late at night?	5	4	3	2	1
Do you get some physical exercise before each meal?	5	4	3	2	1
Do you set aside worries and problems at meal time?	5	4	3	2	1
Do you break an overnight fast each morning with either fresh fruit or fresh fruit juice?	5	4	3	2	1
You can say that your eating habits are regular and consistent.	5	4	3	2	1
You can take the full responsibility for your eating habits.	5	4	3	2	1
You sit down at every meal.	5	4	3	2	1
You consistently under eat and avoid being too full.	5	4	3	2	1
Your eating habits are consistent with what you know are the best eating habits for you.	5	4	3	2	1

Total Points—Eating Habits A:

Scores above 85 are suggestive of an optimal nutritional program.

Scores from 84–74 are within a suboptimal range.
Scores below 73 indicate time for a nutritional wake-up call.

Sound eating habits are the rule for nutritional wellness by doing the following:

- Eating high quality foods
- Being relaxed while eating
- Eating at regular intervals

This is conducive to maximizing the assimilation of what you eat. In the following quiz on eating habits, score 5 for "Never" and 1 for "Always." Upon completion, add your total score. After taking the questionnaire on nutritional habits, see where you can improve your overall program.

Eating Habits B:

	Always	Usually	Sometimes	Rarely	Never
I drink some fluid: water, soda, coffee, tea, milk, wine, or juice with each meal.	1	2	3	4	5
I often think about eating lunch while going through my morning activities.	1	2	3	4	5
I often think about eating dinner while going through my afternoon activities.	1	2	3	4	5
When I am emotionally upset, I usually eat.	1	2	3	4	5
When I am depressed, I usually eat.	1	2	3	4	5

	Always	Usually	Sometimes	Rarely	Never
When I am angry, I usually eat.	1	2	3	4	5
When I am irritable, I usually eat.	1	2	3	4	5
When I am tired, I usually eat.	1	2	3	4	5
I constantly worry about gaining weight.	1	2	3	4	5
I usually snack before going to bed.	1	2	3	4	5
I smoke cigarettes while I eat.	1	2	3	4	5
I read the paper while eating.	1	2	3	4	5
I drink some alcoholic beverages prior to, during, or right after eating.	1	2	3	4	5
I snack on sweet foods between meals.	1	2	3	4	5
I usually overeat, although I know that it is not in my best interest.	1	2	3	4	5
I eat standing up at least once a day.	1	2	3	4	5
I rationalize at least once a day about the quality and quantity of what I eat.	1	2	3	4	5
The first thing I do in the morning when I wake up is think about food.	1	2	3	4	5

Total Points—Eating Habits B:

_____

Scores above 80 are optimal.

Scores below 70 suggest it is time for behavior modification.

Know What Not to Eat

Even more meaningful than what you do eat is knowing what to avoid! Bad foods do more harm than healthy foods do good. Eliminating harmful foods from your program is one of the keys to nutritional balance. It is important to identify and appropriately handle any food addictions such as sugar, salt, cookies, caffeine, fried foods, and chocolate. Remember the following tips:

- Avoid overeating
- Avoid nervous eating habits
- Avoid snacking while cooking
- Avoid eating the last helping just so it won't go to waste
- Avoid eating or drinking while standing, walking, or driving
- Avoid eating when you are emotionally upset, anxious, bored, uptight, depressed, fatigued, or irritable

Take a Stand on the Foods Most Commonly Available

When you eat the right foods in the right proportions, you thrive! Nutritional balance means you are not eating too much or too little of any vital nutrient. Avoid harmful, inferior quality fuel. Nutritional excess and low quality, toxic fuel are very common triggers that cause fatigue, mental wasting, anxiety, and depression, all symptoms of nutritional burnout.

Sugar

Any amount of table sugar is too much. Excess white sugar creates an inefficient, unstable, and faulty metabolism. Refined sugars weaken your liver and adrenal glands, overtax your nerves, and deplete B vitamins. The deficiency state of functional hypoglycemia is often the result. Sweets cause arthritis, premenstrual syndrome, and male and female hormonal dysfunction.

White Flour

Processed, refined (bleached or unbleached) white flour is harmful to your health. White bread has no natural enzyme nutritive value. Eating white bread clogs your digestive track. Eating too much bread puts on weight in the wrong places. White flour also clogs your lymph system and plugs up the filters in your liver, spleen, and lymph nodes.

Salt

Salt in your diet damages your kidneys. It has destructive effects on your stomach as well. Excess salt puts you at high risk for high blood pressure. Do not salt your food.

Refined Carbohydrates

White rice impairs your liver's ability to be the detoxifying machine that it can be. Avoid sweets and artificially sweetened foods. Refined carbohydrates obstruct the natural flow of your lymph system and in turn, increase your susceptibility to cold and flu viruses.

Soft Drinks

They have no nutritional value. Soft drinks are corrosive, highly acidic, and damage your body chemistry. They contain hidden caffeine, sugar, and artificial chemicals. Get real and start drinking natural, fresh squeezed juices and smoothies.

Meats

Avoid meat protein! Red meat is loaded with synthetic chemicals. Meat is a toxic fuel that fills you up artificially and gives you a drugged hyped-up energy level. It hurts your pancreas. Red meat protein consumption results in heavy accumulation of acid residue toxins in the body. This damages nerves and joints. Meat has been cited as a risk factor to the increased incidence in rectal and colon cancer. Eating more animal protein than you need, whether it be meat, fish, or foul, is a negative cultural phenomenon and can be carcinogenic. Read John Robbins' fact-filled *Diet for a New America,* and you will probably never eat meat, fish, or poultry again!

Fats

High fat levels clog the circulation. They are major contributory risk factors for hardening of the arteries, diabetes, stroke, heart disease, and obesity. Excess fat in your diet increases your vulnerability to breast cancer, cancer of the uterus, as well as gall bladder cancer and other malignancies. Too much meat or dairy is a common nutritional turnover. Animal fats, in particular meat and lard, are high in cholesterol. They have negative influence on your hormonal balance.

Milk

Milk is the most exaggerated food in the world for adults and teenagers. Milk is very mucus forming. Pasteurized milk stimulates the upper respiratory passages, ears, nose, throat, sinuses, and the lungs to oversecrete. Pasteurized milk allergies are common. Digestive gland function and assimilation is also compromised from excessive mucus formation.

Caffeine

Caffeine is a social ritual. Overstimulation to the nerves, adrenals, and heart is hazardous to your well being. Headaches, breast lumps, and prostate dysfunction are common results of too much caffeine.

Your Liver and Kidneys Need Your Help

You are smart to avoid the excess of any nutrient that increases your risk to suffer with a diet-related deficiency. Why do I make such a fuss over these frequently-advertised, easy access food items? Because they have a corrosive effect on your liver, kidneys, immune system, and your pancreatic digestive enzymes. The net effect of this pernicious influence is incomplete assimilation and absorption of vital life-giving nutrients.

Eating your way to wellness is an orderly, natural process. It naturally evolves from responsible nutritional decision making. Don't fall victim to eating what is convenient...plenty of sweets, fats, soft drinks, delicatessen meats, chemically processed acid-forming beef, fried chicken, and shellfish. On-the-go nutrition results in nutritional imbalance because of inferior assimilation of minerals, vitamins, and vegetable proteins.

Food Grouping

Before going on, be certain you know what the four major food groups really are and what are the criteria for a balanced maintenance program. The High Performance Living nutritional plan is a balanced maintenance program. Why? Because it provides a truly balanced relationship between complex carbohydrates, simple carbohydrates, proteins, and fats.

The essence of the anti-aging, antioxidant High Performance Living nutritional maintenance program is:

- High in natural hi-enzyme carbohydrates
- Moderate in highly spirited vegetable protein
- Low in high-enzyme natural fats.

High Performance Living Food Grouping

I.   Simple Natural Carbohydrates (fresh fruits, fresh vegetables, and fresh natural juices)—50 percent
II. Whole Complex Carbohydrates (whole grain breads, brown rice, cereals, pastas, and natural starches)—20–25 percent
III. High-quality Proteins (legumes, beans, veggie burgers, tofu, tempeh, etc.)—15–20 percent
IV. Natural Fats (unsaturated oils, unsalted nuts, avocado)—10–15 percent

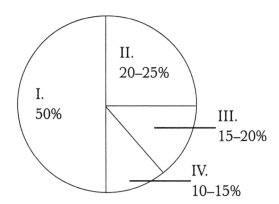

Balanced Maintenance Program

There are twelve main criteria that harmoniously blend together to create the experience of the balanced maintenance program. The ingredients provide the right amount and the right proportions of:

- *High quality simple natural carbohydrates.* 50 percent of the optimal maintenance program (OMP). Your fresh fruits and raw vegetables give you enough of the phyto-nutrients and antioxidants you need.
- *Whole complex carbohydrates.* 20–25 percent of the OMP.
- *High quality protein.* 15–20 percent of the OMP.
- *Vegetable to animal protein.* The ratio of vegetable to animal protein is of the utmost importance. At least 70 percent and as much as 85–100 percent as vegetable protein.
- *Natural fats.* (Nuts, seeds, avocado)—10 percent.
- *Natural unsaturated to saturated fats.* At least 85 percent of the total fat intake of the optimal maintenance program is unsaturated fatty acids.
- *Minerals and vitamins.* Provide calcium, iron, magnesium, chromium, selenium, zinc, manganese, potassium, vitamin E, vitamin C, B vitamins, and other essential vitamins and minerals in substantial quantities to insure optimal nutrition.
- *Raw to cooked foods.* At least 50 percent of the diet as fresh, raw, living food.
- *Alkaline to acid balance.* A ratio of three parts alkaline to two parts acid (3:2). For some individuals as much as 2:1 alkaline to acid.
- *Dietary fiber.* At least 25 grams daily.
- *Color balance.* The optimal maintenance program is creatively aesthetic and visually appealing.
- *Tastes right.* Use natural herbs and condiments to flavor your food so you can look forward to enjoying your meals.

Maintenance Has Enough Protein

The maintenance diet has a substantial amount of complete protein. It is carefully constructed to provide anywhere from 30–60 grams daily to match your needs. In general, most adults require 40–50 grams of complete protein daily to sufficiently maintain their protein requirements. This does not apply to children, teenagers under eighteen, or competitive high performance athletes. Although the cleansing diet is strictly vegetarian, the maintenance program offers you the option to go vegetarian or not. Nevertheless, at least 80 percent of your maintenance protein is of vegetable origin. The lacto-vegetarian (low fat, soy, or rennetless dairy) maintenance diet is the recommended form of the high performance maintenance program. The non-vegetarian alternative is explained under the guidelines of the maintenance diet.

You can be sure you are getting enough protein when you feel good, look good, are energetic, and can sustain a happy, active sex life. Your body needs just the right amount of protein; that is what nutritional balance is all about. Too much protein predisposes you to arthritis and cancer, and not enough protein causes malnutrition and muscle wasting.

The biochemical essence of the high performance maintenance program is to combine raw living food with complete protein at each and every meal. The exposure to a variety of high quality proteins is what sets maintenance apart from cleansing. Cleansing relies on fresh fruits and vegetables and is low in protein (15–25 grams). The maintenance program is moderate in protein levels. As noted, most adults need 35–50 grams of protein at least five to seven days a week.

How will you live without meat? Very well and very happily! The advantage of the complete vegetarian protein is a higher benefit to risk ratio. This way, you get the benefits of protein without having to pay the taxes for eating high fat, chemically-treated animal proteins. Vegetarian nutrition does require effective food combining to make certain you get all the essential amino acids at one meal. All the homework needed to give you complete protein meals that are based on plant and vegetable proteins (that compete with animal protein) is worked out for you below.

Listed below are all your food combinations and choices to create fresh, raw, living food and wholesome complete protein at breakfast, lunch, and dinner. Complete protein combinations are two or more foods that when eaten together provide all the essential amino acids together to create a complete protein. There is a wide variety of acceptable complete protein combinations on the maintenance program.

Complete Protein/Fruit Combinations for Breakfast

A fresh fruit salad with any one of the following will make breakfast into a complete protein meal:

1) 1 oz. unsalted almonds with 2 oz. low fat granola

2) 1–2 tbsp. nut butter (unsalted, almond butter is preferred) with 2 oz. granola

3) 1–2 slices sprouted seven-grain bread with 1–2 tbsp. nut butter

4) 1 oz. almonds with a bowl of seven-grain cereal; oatmeal, millet, bran, cream-of-rye, or cream-of-wheat cereal

5) 1–3 oz. mixed nuts

Note: Lunch can be light, moderate, or heavier depending on your level of activity.

Lightweight Luncheon
Complete Protein Combinations

Option 1

A fruit salad with any one of the following will make a complete protein:

1) 1/2 cup low fat cottage cheese
2) 1/2 cup non-fat soy yogurt
3) 1–3 oz. nuts and seeds
4) Meltzer Lightweight Fruit Smoothie:

Take any fruit salad using appropriate seasonal fruits and blend together with spirulina or 1–2 tbsp. brewer's yeast, 1 tsp. bee pollen, 1 banana, ice, and 1–2 cups of non-concentrated fruit juice, 10 unsalted, roasted almonds (optional).

Option 2

A leafy-green chlorophyll salad plus any one of the following will make a complete protein:

1) Raw carrots, peas, mushrooms, and 2 tsp. sunflower seeds added to a salad
2) Raw carrots, peas, cauliflower, and 2 tsp. sunflower seeds added to a salad
3) 1/2 cup steamed carrots, 1/2 cup steamed peas, 8 medium mushrooms, and 2 tsp. sunflower seeds added to a salad
4) 1 cup steamed green vegetables in season with 2 tsp. sunflower seeds added to a salad
5) Avocado inside a heated corn tortilla for a veggie guacamole taco

Welterweight Luncheon
Complete Protein Combinations

A leafy-green chlorophyll salad plus any one of the following will make a complete protein:

1) Tabbouleh with 2 tsp. sunflower seeds added to the salad
2) Tofu salad with tofu, celery, onions, and tomato
3) Lima bean soup with 2 tsp. sunflower seeds in the salad
4) Bean vegetable soup with 2 tsp. sunflower seeds in the salad
5) Split pea soup with 2 tsp. sunflower seeds in the salad
6) Mushroom or carrot-onion soup with sunflower or sesame seeds in the salad
7) Lentil soup with 2 tsp. sunflower seeds in a salad
8) Potato salad (eggless) with 2 tsp. sunflower seeds in a salad
9) Potato-leek soup with cottage cheese (1/2 cup) with a salad
10) Guacamole on carrot or celery sticks
11) Vegetarian taco—fresh raw or steamed vegetables inside a warm corn tortilla. Avocado can be added
12) Avocado sandwich on 2 slices of sprouted seven-grain bread
13) Mid-eastern garbanzo spread (hummus) with whole wheat pita pocket bread

Heavyweight Luncheon
Complete Protein Combinations

(Be certain to earn these meals)

A leafy-green chlorophyll salad plus any one of the following will make a complete protein:

1) Avocado sandwich on 2 slices of sprouted seven-grain bread and mixed vegetable soup
2) The pita stuff: avocado, tomato, sprouts, and onions inside whole wheat pita bread, and mixed vegetable soup
3) Lentil soup with 1–2 slices sprouted seven-grain bread
4) Guacamole with vegetable bean soup
5) Guacamole taco: a corn tortilla or whole wheat chapati without cheese and mixed vegetable soup
6) Quesadilla: a corn tortilla with rennetless or soy based cheese, with or without mixed vegetable soup
7) Falafel: a garbanzo bean patty inside whole wheat pita bread
8) Veggie burger: mushroom, soy, lentil, garbanzo, or tofu burger without bread with vegetable soup
9) Veggie burger with a whole wheat bun
10) Split pea soup with 1–2 slices sprouted seven-grain or whole wheat pita bread
11) Bean vegetable soup with 1–2 slices sprouted seven-grain or whole wheat pita bread

Complete Protein Dinner Combinations

A leafy-green chlorophyll salad with any one of the following choices from A1 to F5 will make a complete protein:

(** indicates recipes given at the end of this chapter)

A. Complete Soybean Combinations

1) Scrambled tofu with vegetables.** Scrambled tofu with brown or wild rice
2) Tofu chop suey with vegetarian egg rolls**
3) Tofu lasagna (use your favorite lasagna recipe but substitute soy cheese for cheese and use scrambled tofu instead of meat)

4) Vegetable casserole (soybeans and vegetables on brown rice)
5) Soy burger on whole grain bun
6) Tempeh burger on whole grain bun
7) Soy cheeseburger on a whole grain bun (use soy cheese)
8) Soy grits with 1/2 cup of cooked brown rice and 1/2 cup of soy milk
9) Whole grain pasta (noodles with tofu and fresh tomato sauce)

B. Complete Bean Combinations

1) Organic tostada: corn tortilla, 1/2 cup cooked beans (kidney and pinto), sprouts, tomato
2) Falafel: 1/4 cup garbanzo beans made into a patty combined with mushrooms, onions, green bell pepper, and sesame seeds with or without pita bread
3) Hummus Lebanese dip: 1/2 cup cooked garbanzo bean spread, 1/2 slices whole wheat pita
4) Beans and rice: mung beans, adzuki beans, lima beans, kidney beans, pinto beans with brown or wild rice, 1/2 cup each
5) Vegetarian enchiladas, burritos, or tamales

C. Complete Soup and Grain Combinations

1) Lima bean vegetable soup with 1–2 slices whole grain bread
2) Lima bean vegetable soup with brown rice
3) Split pea soup with 1/2 cup brown or wild rice
4) Split pea soup with 1–2 slices whole grain or whole wheat pita bread
5) Minestrone bean vegetable soup with 1/2 cup brown rice

6) Minestrone bean vegetable soup with 1–2 slices whole grain bread
7) Whole grain pasta noodles with tomato sauce and mushroom soup
8) Whole grain pasta noodles with fresh tomato sauce, mixed with scrambled tofu and vegetable soup

D. Complete Lentil Combinations

1) Lentil mixed vegetable soup with raw or sautéed mushrooms
2) Lentil mushroom vegetable casserole with sesame or sunflower seeds in the salad
3) Lentil sesame nut roast
4) Lentil soup with 1–2 slices whole grain or whole wheat pita bread**
5) Lentil soup with 1/2 cup brown rice or millet
6) Lentil burger on whole wheat bun

E. Complete Pea Combinations

1) Steamed peas, steamed carrots, 1 baked potato with 2 tsp. sesame seeds added to a salad
2) Vegetable casserole and sesame seeds (2 tsp.) added to a salad**

F. Vegetable-Cheese Casseroles

(use soy cheese or rennetless cheese)
1) Veggie lasagna
2) Eggplant parmesan
3) Vegetarian pizza
4) Zucchini-rice casseroles with or without cheese
5) Vegetarian enchiladas

Blueprint for the High Performance Living Nutritional Maintenance Program

The maintenance program provides you with substantial amounts of essential, complete protein that you need to stay in good health.

Morning. Twenty minutes of aerobics, deep breathing, and hydrotherapy, followed by fifteen minutes of meditation and The Maintenance Breakfast.

The Maintenance Breakfast

Fresh fruit juice in season (6 oz.)

Fifteen minutes later:
Fresh fruit salad
Complete protein fruit combinations
Alfalfa sprouts—optional (as many as you want)

Mid-day. Sunshine, fresh air, recharge your body, stretch, clear your mind, followed by The Maintenance Lunch.

For those who have exerted themselves physically as well as mentally, a heavyweight luncheon is sometimes needed. For those who have exerted themselves mentally and not physically, at the best, a welterweight lunch is needed. For those that have neither exerted themselves physically or mentally, a lightweight luncheon will suffice.

The Maintenance Lunch

Lightweight
Option 1:
  Fruit salad with lightweight fruit
  Complete protein combination

The Maintenance Lunch (cont'd)
Option 2:
Leafy-green chlorophyll salad with herbal dressing
Lightweight vegetable complete protein combination
Welterweight
Leafy-green chlorophyll salad with herbal dressing
Welterweight luncheon complete protein combination
Heavyweight
Leafy-green chlorophyll salad with herbal dressing
Heavyweight luncheon complete protein combination

Evening. Fifteen minutes of yoga or t'ai chi and meditation followed by The Maintenance Dinner.

The Maintenance Dinner
Fresh raw carrot juice, carrot-celery juice, or carrot-celery-beet juice.
Fifteen minutes later:
Leafy-green chlorophyll salad with your choice of herbal salad dressing
One complete protein dinner combination from A1 to F6.

Guidelines for the Maintenance Program

To give you an overview of the foods recommended on the maintenance diet, check out what's in and what's out!

The foods recommended are:

Seasonal Fresh Fruits and Fruit Juices	yes	All fresh fruits in season, fresh fruit salad at breakfast. Fruit salad option available for

		lightweight lunch. Emphasis on apples, cantaloupe, watermelon, papaya, grapes, oranges, bananas, grapefruit, peaches. Dried fruits in moderation for social occasions.
Fresh Vegetables and Raw Vegetable Juices	yes	All fresh vegetables with an emphasis on romaine lettuce, sprouts, mushrooms, fresh peas, celery, carrots, avocado, cauliflower, spinach, tomatoes, red onions, cucumber. Steamed broccoli, zucchini, string bean, and eggplant are of significance.
Sprouts	yes	Emphasize alfalfa and bean sprouts with your raw salads.
Nuts	yes	Almonds, walnuts, and cashews in moderation. Pecans, brazil nuts, and macadamia nuts for special occasions. Absolutely no salt.
Nut Butters	yes	Peanut butter, cashew butter, almond butter, sesame-tahini butter, unsalted and un-hydrogenated in moderation.
Seeds	yes	Sunflower, sesame, and pumpkin seeds as a garnish to your vegetable salad.

Whole Grains	yes	Whole-grain cereals optional at breakfast. Whole grain breads optional at lunch. Cooked whole grain suggested at dinner. Eat whole grains for two meals a day.
Legumes	yes	Tofu, soy burgers, beans, peas, and lentils are very good staples.
Dairy Products	yes	Rennetless or soy cheese, low fat cottage cheese, low fat soy yogurt are suggested in moderation (up to once a day, no more than two to three times a week).
	yes	Raw, rennetless cheese is the preferred cheese because it is less mucus forming.
	no	Avoid all pasteurized, processed, colored hard cheeses
Eggs, Yogurt, Milk	no	Eggs, yogurt, and milk are very mucus forming.
Beverages	yes	Herbal teas of choice. Fresh fruit juice, fruit smoothies, and fresh carrot juice (8 oz.) or other fresh raw vegetable juices.
Seasonings	yes	Cleansing herbs, basic herbs, salsa

Flesh Foods: Meat	no	The non-vegetarian alternative to the Meltzer maintenance diet is organic white meat of turkey without skin, organic white meat of chicken without skin, broiled or baked fish (except shellfish) not more than once a day and up to two to three times a week.

A Typical Day in the Life of Your Maintenance Plan

Study the blueprint below to select and combine your food when sticking to Dr. Meltzer's high performance nutritional maintenance program.

High Performance Living Maintenance Breakfast

7:00–8:00 A.M.

Select one of the following fruit salads according to the season:

Spring

Orange juice (6 oz.)

Fifteen minutes later:
South American Tropical Fruit Salad
- 1/2 cup papaya
- medium banana
- 1/2 cup pineapple

Almonds (1/2 oz.) with seven-grain cereal or oatmeal (1/2 bowl)

Summer

Papaya juice (6 oz.)

Fifteen minutes later:
Summer Melon Salad
- 1/2 medium cantaloupe
- 1/2 cup watermelon
- 1/2 cup honeydew

Seven-grain sprouted toast, 1–2 slices with almond butter

Autumn

Apple juice (6 oz.)

Fifteen minutes later:
Autumn Salad
- 1/2 medium Fuji apple
- 1/2 cup papaya
- 1 medium banana

Whole grain toast with almond butter, 1–2 slices

Winter

Orange juice (6 oz.)

Fifteen minutes later:
Papaya Salad
- 1/2 medium orange
- 1/2 cup papaya
- 1 medium banana

Whole grain toast with almond butter, 1–2 slices

High Performance Living Maintenance Luncheon

12:30–2:00 P.M.

Lightweight

Leafy-Green Chlorophyll Salad
Herbal dressing
1/2 cup steamed carrots
1/2 cup steamed peas
8 medium mushrooms
2 tsp. sunflower seeds in salad

Welterweight

Leafy-Green Chlorophyll Salad
Herbal dressing
Mighty Mushroom Carrot-Onion Soup with 1-2 tsp.
   sunflower seeds added to salad

Heavyweight

Garden Pea Salad
Herbal dressing
Soy burger on whole wheat bun

High Performance Living Maintenance Dinner

5:30–7:00 P.M.

Fresh carrot, carrot-celery, or carrot-celery-beet juice (8 oz.).

Fifteen minutes later:
Spice-of-Life Spinach Salad
  • 4 leaves spinach
  • 2–4 leaves romaine lettuce
  • 1/4 medium red onion
  • 1/2 large tomato
  • 1 stalk celery

- 1/2 cup alfalfa sprouts
- 2 tsp. sesame or sunflower seeds

Herbal dressing

Vegetarian Lasagna

When You Travel or Go Out

When you are traveling, keep an open mind. With seeing eyes, you can stay as close to the program as possible. Seek out the best natural foods restaurants. Ask around and look under specialized dining directories to find the best places to eat. When you go out to eat, especially when you are with friends, enjoy yourself!

Be certain to place the highest priority on loving, sharing communication with those breaking bread with you. Have fun! The food you are eating is not the main reason you are out with friends and loved ones. When people ask you why you are not indulging in their kind of food and drink, simply respond that you feel better eating what appeals to you. With a smile on your face and light in your eyes, tell them you really enjoy what you choose to eat. Just be mellow and calm about it.

With some creativity, persistence, and enthusiasm, you can generally find some high quality restaurants. It often boils down to your personal values and what kind of nutrition suits you best. Absolutely draw the lines on what you will not eat! Then within the boundaries of what you select to eat, enjoy! Don't be difficult. Most Italian, Chinese, and Indian restaurants have a wide variety of vegetarian entrees. Even the most traditional restaurants serve fresh salads, garden vegetables, and baked potatoes.

One word about cheating while on this program...as we were taught in grade school, the only person you really cheat when you are cheating is yourself. To get the main benefits of this nutritional plan, the closer you follow it, the greater the results. As you get in touch with your own nutritional and emotional needs, you become more of an expert in determining what your optimal nutritional plan is. Continuity and consistency make all the difference. Keep cool. Be discrete. Stay relaxed and centered. Then you will know what to do.

Nutritional Supplements for Maintenance

Nutritional supplements can be important adjuncts in rounding out your maintenance plan. The essence of your high performance nutritional program is to rely on your food choices rather than vitamin supplements to provide you with your nutritional needs. However, it is almost impossible to eat only fresh, organic food. It is a fact of life that our soils have been nutritionally depleted, our air and water sources are polluted, and many commonly available foods are treated with chemicals. Therefore, I do recommend a comprehensive, all-purpose, multi-vitamin, multi-mineral supplement to fortify your nutritional plan. I recommend Re-Vita (liquid spirulina) due to its high level of bio-availability. This means the Re-Vita gets absorbed and assimilated with superior efficiency.

Given the level of stress and environmental toxicity in modern day society, I also recommend an antioxidant supplement. For those over the age of forty-five, antioxidant therapy is well-advised. At age fifty-five or older, they are obligatory to protect your heart, liver, tissues, and eyes from degeneration. Use these guidelines for antioxidant therapy.

Antioxidants to Supplement Your Program

Vitamin E	400 units	3 x day
Selenium	200 mcg.	2 x day
Co-enzyme Q	60 mg.	2 x day
Zinc	50 mg.	2 x day
Glutathione	50 mg.	2 x day
Pycnogenol	60 mg.	2 x day
Curcuminoids (Curcumin)	250 mg.	2 x day
Beta Carotene in the form of mixed carotenoids	50,000 units	1 x day

Most certainly, there are ample opportunities to get enough vitamin B-12 on the maintenance diet. With your consumption of sunflower seeds, bananas, peanut butter, bee pollen, dairy products, kelp, tempeh, or spirulina, you can be certain to get enough B-12.

All the prepared food combinations and meals in this program have their recipes spelled out in *Dr. Meltzer's 21-day Del Mar Diet Book*. Below are some sample recipes to get you started. Good Luck and Bon Appetit!

Tofu Chop Suey

1/2 cup celery, chopped
1 large onion, chopped
1 tbsp. safflower oil
1 cup mushrooms, chopped
1 cup mung bean sprouts
1/2 cup Chinese cabbage
Cubed tofu (1/2 lb.)

Sauté onion and celery in oil until almost soft. Add mushrooms, sprouts, and cabbage. Toss and sauté for 3–5 minutes. Add tofu to heat. Serve over brown rice if desired. A small dash of tamari adds extra flavor. 1 tsp. minced ginger may be added while you sauté the vegetables. Broccoli, snow peas, or sesame seeds are other optional additions.

Brown Rice

Short, medium, or long grain can be mixed together. Wild rice can be added and cooked with other rice for added flavor. Add 1 bay leaf with your favorite herbs, such as dill and onion or add a vegetable bouillon cube or tamari to the rice. As a rule of thumb, 1 part rice to 2 parts water. Cook 40–50 minutes. Cooked rice is $2^{1}/_{2}$ times the quantity of uncooked rice.

Lentil Soup

1 cup dry lentils
1 bay leaf
2 cups water
1 carrot, sliced
2–3 tomatoes, blended with scant water
1 red onion, chopped
8 mushrooms, sliced
1 stalk celery, chopped

Seasonings of choice: dill, ginger, cumin, cayenne, basil (1/4 tsp. each), 2 cloves garlic.

Cook lentils and bay leaf in 2 cups water for 30 minutes. Add balance of ingredients and simmer until lentils are tender.

Vegetable Casserole

1 cup zucchini, sliced
1 cup broccoli florets
1 cup carrots, sliced
1/4 cup onion, chopped
2 tbsp. parsley, chopped
1 cup cold water
2 tomatoes, chopped
1/2 cup brown rice, raw

Steam lightly zucchini, broccoli, and carrots. Cook remaining ingredients with brown rice for 40 minutes. Place alternate layers of steamed vegetables and rice mixture in casserole. Heat in 325° oven for 15 minutes.

Scrambled Tofu

3 tbsp. safflower oil (unrefined)
1 onion, diced
5 cloves garlic, crushed
2 cups tofu, cut into cubes
12 mushrooms, chopped
1 tbsp. fresh ginger, grated (optional)
herbs (i.e., spike, tamari)

In a large skillet heat oil. Sauté onion and garlic until golden brown. Add tofu. Cover and steam in own juices, stirring often. Uncover, let brown, add mushrooms and seasonings. Cover and cook briefly. Other vegetables may be included for vegetable chow mein. Serve over brown rice.

Develop the Habit of Physical Fitness and Keep Metabolically Fit

PHYSICAL FITNESS is defined by sustained energy, vitality, stamina, and aerobic conditioning. Furthermore, when you are physically fit, you are agile and strong and have the ability to successfully meet the challenges of a demanding daily routine with enthusiasm and vigor. When you are in shape, your resting heart rate is about sixty and your heart, lungs, and arteries are in fine working order.

The benefits of invigorating exercise include more energy, higher spirits, a better self-esteem, and improved digestion. It also serves as an antitoxin to fight physical and mental fatigue and is an effective antidote to emotional and physical stress. A daily fitness program enhances sexual vitality, builds your confidence, and ensures that you sleep more soundly.

A regular exercise routine is a prerequisite to a sound and efficient metabolism. Your metabolism is the rate at which you burn fat. It is also the biochemical manifestation of your body chemistries. The habit of daily physical fitness keeps you metabolically proficient. This will keep you in line with your ideal body weight. All in all, physical fitness is a necessary component to High Performance Living, which inspires your mind and body connection and takes it to the next level.

Consistent exercise is a special tonic that has magical healing powers on the heart. Did you know that each day your heart can beat as many as one hundred thousand times and pump as much as two thousand gallons of blood throughout your body? Your heart needs the exercise of love and the love of exercise to create High Performance Living.

Cardiovascular fitness gets your circulation into shape. A healthy circulation requires a vital, responsive, dynamic heart muscle with resilient, obedient, attending blood vessels. This happens when the heart, blood vessels, arteries, veins, and capillaries are conditioned through steady and consistent exercise.

Fit individuals have a built-in mechanism to control their eating habits, especially overeating. Therefore, physical fitness decreases your mental appetite for the overloading of your body. When you are not in top shape, you often have a driving appetite for sweets, pastries, breads, and animal protein, not a real need for them. Psychologically revved up appetites are deleterious to your health and are the result of weak nerves. Regular exercise puts you in touch with your real needs for food and fuel by strengthening your nerves, willpower, and heart.

Regular exercise has been shown to favorably modify elevated blood fat and blood cholesterol levels. A consistent routine can modify high blood pressure and prevent obesity. It also maintains your blood sugar at a more constant level. This metabolic fitness prevents low blood sugar and diabetes. In addition to looking better, regular exercise has a most beneficial effect on your brain chemistry. It is the most natural anti-depressant known to man. When you are fit, you feel great and slow down your aging process. The neuroendorphins released into your bloodstream during regular exercise strengthen your mind/body connection.

Take the following assessment of your present condition. Then, depending on your level, gradually begin training, but not straining. The more advanced you are, clearly the greater the intensity, duration, and frequency of your program. Similarly, beginners will need to build up to higher levels. Do not ever get discouraged; forge ahead!

Physical Fitness Self-Assessment

Determine your level of physical fitness at present. Score: 4 for "Always," 3 for "Usually," 2 for "Sometimes," 1 for "Rarely," 0 for "Never." Tally your score.

	Always	Usually	Sometimes	Rarely	Never
I jog, swim, cycle, jump rope, or do aerobic dancing at least fifteen minutes every day.	4	3	2	1	0
I practice stretching exercises and/or calisthenics every day.	4	3	2	1	0
I practice balancing exercises, yoga, t'ai chi, kung fu, or recharging for fifteen minutes every day.	4	3	2	1	0
I walk at least three miles every day.	4	3	2	1	0
I play tennis, racquetball, or other sports as recreational activities at least two times a week.	4	3	2	1	0

	Always	Usually	Sometimes	Rarely	Never
I take the time each day to keep physically fit.	4	3	2	1	0
I work up a good sweat at least once a day.	4	3	2	1	0
I perform sustained physical labor such as chopping wood, lifting heavy objects, working in the garden, using mechanical tools, or other vigorous physical work every day.	4	3	2	1	0
I walk up stairs instead of using an elevator at every opportunity.	4	3	2	1	0
My physical endurance is increasing on a daily basis.	4	3	2	1	0
My spinal flexibility is increasing on a daily basis.	4	3	2	1	0
My muscle power and strength are increasing on a daily basis.	4	3	2	1	0
I can run $1\frac{1}{2}$ miles in twelve minutes, I can swim 500 yards in ten minutes, or I can cycle 3 miles in fifteen minutes.	4	3	2	1	0
I can walk 3/4 mile in twelve minutes.	4	3	2	1	0
I can do twelve pushups.	4	3	2	1	0
I can lift my own body weight.	4	3	2	1	0

	Always	Usually	Sometimes	Rarely	Never
I can hold the t'ai chi horse stance for three minutes.	4	3	2	1	0
When I wake up in the morning, my body is ready for a workout.	4	3	2	1	0
I can exercise for thirty minutes continuously without having to take a break.	4	3	2	1	0
I can do twenty complete sit-ups.	4	3	2	1	0
I can touch my toes without bending my knees.	4	3	2	1	0
I can walk up three flights of stairs (twenty-five steps to a flight) without getting short of breath.	4	3	2	1	0
I spend more time walking each day than I do driving or as a passenger in a car.	4	3	2	1	0
I can sit in a semi-lotus or full-lotus position with my back straight for at least five minutes without experiencing fatigue or any back pain.	4	3	2	1	0
I have been without neck pain or muscle aches for at least eighteen months.	4	3	2	1	0
I practice risk exercises* at least once a week.	4	3	2	1	0

* Risk exercises are activities with added risk, for example, surfing, horseback riding, skiing, hiking in the mountains, etc.

Total Points:

_____

86–96 points   advanced
65–85 points   intermediate
Less than 64   beginning

Lifestyle Convenience Assessment

Can you alter some of your activities to incorporate more exercise?

Can you walk to the Post Office, movie theaters, shopping center?

Can you climb the stairs instead of taking the elevators, etc?

Golden Rules for Feeling Tops while Exercising

Rule #1 Enjoy!
Rule #2 Have fun and look forward to exercising!
Rule #3 Approach your program with enthusiasm!
Rule #4 Proper posture and breathing will enhance your efficiency!
Rule #5 Make it a regular habit!

Components of a Comprehensive Physical Fitness Program

There are seven components to the comprehensive fitness program inherent in High Performance Living. They are:

- Aerobic Conditioning
- Spinal Flexibility
- Recharging Exercises
- Strengthening Exercises
- Endurance Training
- Recreational Exercise
- Risk Exercises

Aerobic Conditioning

Sustained aerobic activity generates enough oxygen to appropriately condition your cardiovascular system. Aerobics include jogging, speed walking, cycling, swimming, jumping rope, aerobic dance, and cross-country skiing. The key is sustained, uninterrupted, vigorous exercise.

The prescription for your aerobic conditioning has three phases:

A. Warm-up period: about five minutes of low-key stretching, joint rotations, sit-ups, push-ups, or salutation to the sun (hatha-yoga). End with trotting in place with deep nostril breathing.

B. Fifteen to twenty minutes of sustained vigorous exercise, reaching at least twelve to fifteen minutes at your Target Heart Rate (THR). To calculate your THR, subtract your age from 220 to get your maximum heart rate. Your THR is 60–80 percent of your maximum heart rate. For example, at age forty, your maximum heart rate is 220 - 40 = 180. Therefore 60–80 percent of 180 is 109–144 beats per minute as your THR. That is what you want to sustain for twelve to fifteen minutes.

C. Cool-down period: gently bring the heart rate down with a slow walk and gentle stretching for at least five minutes.

Sample Aerobic Conditioning Program
Jogging—Beginning Level

Week 1   Walk 2/3 mile in twenty minutes daily. Work up to it. This is the goal for the end of the week. 75 percent of the time should be on a flat surface and 25 percent walking up hills or up an incline.

Week 2   Walk 1 mile in thirty minutes.

Week 3   Walk 1¼ miles in thirty minutes

Week 4   Walk 1½ miles in thirty minutes on Monday, Wednesday, Friday, and Sunday. On Tuesday, Thursday, and Saturday, alternate walking for five minutes and jogging for one minute for a total of thirty minutes.

Week 5   Walk 1¾ miles in thirty minutes on Monday, Wednesday, Friday, and Sunday. On Tuesday, Thursday, and Saturday, walk five minutes, jog three minutes, for a total of thirty minutes. Alternate walking and jogging at a very gradual pace.

Week 6   On Monday, Wednesday, Friday, and Sunday, walk 2 miles in thirty minutes. On Tuesday, Thursday, and Saturday, alternate walking for five minutes and jogging for five minutes.

Week 7   Walk 1/4 mile in four minutes, jog 1/4 mile in four minutes, walk 1/4 mile in four minutes, jog 1/4 mile in four minutes, for thirty to thirty-five minutes on Monday, Wednesday, Friday, and Sunday. Walk 1/4 mile in four minutes, but jog 1/4 mile in three minutes; walk 1/4 mile in four minutes, jog 1/4 mile in three minutes, for thirty minutes on Tuesday, Thursday, and Saturday.

Week 8   Walk 1/4 mile in four minutes, jog 1/2 mile in six minutes, Repeat this daily for thirty minutes.

Jogging—Intermediate Level

Week 1	Walk 1/4 mile in four minutes, jog 3/4 mile in ten minutes. Repeat. Then end with slow-down walk for five minutes. Repeat daily.
Week 2	Walk 1/4 mile in three minutes, forty-five seconds, jog 1 mile in twelve minutes. Repeat daily.
Week 3	Walk 1/4 mile in three minutes, forty-five seconds, jog 1 mile in twelve minutes. Repeat daily.
Week 4	Jog 1 mile in twelve minutes, then 1/2 mile in seven minutes, then walk 1/2 mile in eight minutes. When time permits, repeat this.
Week 5	Jog 1 mile in twelve minutes, then 1 mile in fourteen minutes, then jog 1 mile in twelve minutes, for a total of 3 miles daily.
Week 6	Jog 1 mile in twelve minutes, then 1 mile in eleven minutes, then jog 1 mile in eleven minutes, for a total of 3 miles daily.
Week 7	Jog 3 miles in thirty-three minutes daily.
Week 8	Jog 1 mile in ten minutes, then 1 mile in eleven minutes, then jog 1 mile in ten minutes, for a total of 3 miles daily.

Jogging—Advanced Level

Week 1	Jog 3 miles in thirty minutes daily.
Week 2	Jog 3 miles in twenty-nine minutes, thirty seconds daily.
Week 3	Jog 3 miles in twenty-nine minutes.
Week 4	Jog 3 miles in twenty-five minutes, thirty seconds.
Week 5	Jog 3 miles in twenty-eight minutes.
Week 6	Jog 3 miles in twenty-seven minutes.
Week 7	Jog 3 miles in twenty-six minutes.
Week 8	Jog 3 miles in twenty-five minutes.

Once established, maintain jogging 2 miles four times a week in twenty minutes, 2 miles two times a week for sixteen minutes, and 1 mile once a week at ten to twelve minutes.

For guidelines on swimming, cycling, and walking, see the end of this chapter.

Spinal Flexibility

Hatha-yoga is the exercise of choice for keeping your spine, neck, and back loose and relaxed. Yoga means union, of mind, body, and spirit. Hatha-yoga stretches joints, tendons, ligaments, and muscles. It is recommended to have an instructor and take a few classes to get your yoga routine into gear. When yoga is combined with breathing techniques and concentration, it becomes a complete healing meditation. It is recommended to practice your flexibility program on a daily basis.

Recharging Exercises

Activity that immediately arouses and activates your energy level. T'ai chi, kung fu, or calisthenics are all good and should be done daily. The idea is to draw energy and strength into your body. Take the time to recharge before breakfast and dinner to energize your lifestyle.

Strengthening Exercises

Strengthen your body with weights at the gym or at home three times a week for twenty minutes. This will give you a stronger body and will build lean muscle mass.

Endurance Training

Give yourself one to two times a week for a prolonged walk, run, cycle, swim, or difficult hike. This will help your stamina.

Recreational Exercise

Play tennis, volleyball, basketball, golf, or do t'ai chi for balance as often as you can.

Risk Exercises

Activities with added risk make you appreciate being alive. Enjoy backpacking, mountain climbing, surfing, and horseback riding as often as possible.

Physical Fitness Checklist

Before you take your first step in your exercise program, review and initial the information below:

> I understand all the benefits of exercise.
> I am prepared to make a commitment to work out each day and create the positive habit of daily physical fitness.
> I will take the responsibility to find out what kinds of exercise I enjoy.
> I realize that to get physically fit, I need to want it, taste it, and work for it regardless of the weather, my travels, professional life, etc.

The habit of physical fitness will not let you down. Take a look at the following training regimens for swimming, cycling, and walking. Select the program that is most compatible with your personality and needs.

Guidelines for Swimming, Cycling, and Walking

Swimming—Beginning Level

Week 1	Walk 3/4 mile in twenty minutes; swim 100 yards in two minutes, forty-five seconds
Week 2	Walk 3/4 mile in seventeen minutes, thirty seconds; swim 150 yards in four minutes
Week 3	Walk 3/4 mile in fifteen minutes; swim 175 yards in four minutes, forty seconds
Week 4	Walk 3/4 mile in fifteen minutes; swim 200 yards in five minutes, thirty seconds

Week 5   Walk 3/4 mile in fourteen minutes; swim 225 yards in six minutes, then swim slowly for fourteen minutes, for a total of twenty minutes

Week 6   Swim 250 yards in six minutes, thirty seconds; swim slowly for about thirteen minutes, thirty seconds (remainder of twenty minutes)

Week 7   Swim 250 yards in six minutes; swim slowly for fourteen minutes

Week 8   Swim 300 yards in seven minutes; swim slowly for thirteen minutes

Week 9   Swim 325 yards in seven minutes, thirty seconds; swim slowly for twelve minutes, thirty seconds

Week 10   Swim 350 yards in eight minutes; swim slowly for twelve minutes

Week 11   Swim 375 yards in eight minutes, thirty seconds; swim slowly for eleven minutes, thirty seconds

Week 12   Swim 400 yards in nine minutes; swim slowly for eleven minutes

Swimming—Intermediate Level

Week 1   Swim 250 yards in six minutes; swim slowly for fourteen minutes, for a total of twenty minutes

Week 2   Swim 300 yards in seven minutes; swim slowly for thirteen minutes

Week 3   Swim 325 yards in seven minutes, thirty seconds; swim slowly for twelve minutes, thirty seconds

Week 4   Swim 350 yards in eight minutes; swim slowly for twelve minutes

Week 5   Swim 375 yards in eight minutes, thirty seconds; swim slowly for eleven minutes, thirty seconds

Week 6   Swim 400 yards in nine minutes; swim slowly for eleven minutes

Week 7   Swim 450 yards in ten minutes; swim slowly for ten minutes

Week 8   Swim 500 yards in eleven minutes; swim slowly for nine minutes

Week 9   Swim 550 yards in twelve minutes; swim slowly for eight minutes

Week 10   Swim 600 yards in thirteen minutes; swim slowly for seven minutes

Week 11   Swim 650 yards in fourteen minutes; swim slowly for six minutes

Week 12   Swim 700 yards in fifteen minutes; swim slowly for five minutes

Swimming—Advanced Level

Week 1   Swim 750 yards in sixteen minutes

Week 2   Swim 800 yards in seventeen minutes

Week 3   Swim 825 yards in seventeen minutes, thirty seconds

Week 4   Swim 850 yards in eighteen minutes

Week 5   Swim 875 yards in eighteen minutes, thirty seconds

Week 6   Swim 900 yards in nineteen minutes

Week 7   Swim 900 yards in eighteen minutes, forty-five seconds

Week 8   Swim 900 yards in eighteen minutes, thirty seconds

Week 9   Swim 900 yards in eighteen minutes, fifteen seconds

Week 10   Swim 900 yards in eighteen minutes

Week 11   Swim 900 yards in seventeen minutes, forty-five seconds

Week 12   Swim 900 yards in seventeen minutes, thirty seconds

Thereafter, swim 900 yards in seventeen minutes, thirty seconds, four times a week; swim 600 yards between twelve and fourteen minutes, two times a week; and swim 500 yards in twelve minutes, thirty seconds, once a week.

Cycling—Beginning Level

Week 1   Walk 3/4 mile in twenty minutes, seven days a week; cycle 2 miles in twelve minutes, seven days a week

Week 2   Walk 3/4 mile in seventeen minutes, thirty seconds, seven days a week; cycle 2 miles in eleven minutes, seven days a week

Week 3   Walk 1 mile in twenty minutes, seven days a week; cycle 2 miles in eleven minutes, seven days a week

Week 4   Walk 1 mile in eighteen minutes, seven days a week; cycle 3 miles in sixteen minutes, seven days a week

Week 5   Walk 1/2 mile in nine minutes, seven days a week; cycle 4 miles in eighteen minutes, seven days a week

Week 6   Cycle 5 miles in twenty-two minutes, thirty seconds, seven days a week

Week 7   Cycle 5 miles in twenty minutes, six days a week; cycle 5 miles in twenty-four minutes, one day a week

Week 8   Cycle 5 miles in nineteen minutes, six days a week; cycle 5 miles in twenty-three minutes, one day a week

Week 9   Cycle 5 miles in eighteen minutes, thirty seconds, six days a week; cycle 5 miles in twenty-three minutes, one day a week

Week 10   Cycle 5 miles in eighteen minutes, six days a week; cycle 5 miles in twenty-two minutes, one day a week

Week 11   Cycle 6 miles in twenty-five minutes, six days a week; cycle 6 miles in thirty-one minutes, one day a week

Week 12   Cycle 6 miles in twenty-four minutes, six days a week; cycle 6 miles in thirty minutes, one day a week

Cycling—Intermediate Level

Week 1   Cycle 5 miles in twenty minute, six days a week; cycle 5 miles in twenty-five minutes, one day a week

Week 2   Cycle 5 miles in nineteen minutes, six days a week; cycle 5 miles in twenty-four minutes, one day a week

Week 3   Cycle 5 miles in eighteen minutes, thirty seconds, six days a week; cycle 5 miles in twenty-three minutes, one day a week

Week 4   Cycle 5 miles in eighteen minutes, six days a week; cycle 5 miles in twenty-two minutes, one day a week

Week 5   Cycle 6 miles in twenty-five minutes, six days a week; cycle 6 miles in thirty minutes, one day a week

Week 6   Cycle 6 miles in twenty-four minutes, six days a week; cycles 6 miles in thirty minutes, one day a week

Week 7   Cycle 6 miles in twenty-two minutes, thirty seconds, six days a week; cycle 5 miles in seventeen minutes, one day a week

Week 8   Cycle 6 miles in twenty-two minutes, six days a week; cycle 5 miles in seventeen minutes, one day a week

Week 9   Cycle 6 miles in twenty-one minutes, thirty seconds, six days a week; cycle 5 miles in sixteen minutes, thirty seconds, one day a week

Week 10   Cycle 6 miles in twenty-one minutes, six days a week; cycle 5 miles in sixteen minutes, two days a week

Week 11   Cycle 7 miles in twenty-four minutes, thirty seconds, six days a week; cycle 6 miles in twenty-one minutes, one day a week

Week 12   Cycle 7 miles in twenty-four minutes, six days a week; cycle 6 miles in twenty minutes, one day a week

Cycling—Advanced Level

Week 1   Cycle 7 miles in twenty-three minutes, forty-five seconds

Week 2   Cycle 7 miles in twenty-three minutes, thirty seconds

Week 3   Cycle 7 miles in twenty-three minutes, fifteen seconds

Week 4   Cycle 7 miles in twenty-three minutes
Week 5   Cycle 7 miles in twenty-two minutes, forty-five seconds
Week 6   Cycle 7 miles in twenty-two minutes, thirty seconds
Week 7   Cycle 7 miles in twenty-two minutes, fifteen seconds
Week 8   Cycle 7 miles in twenty-two minutes
Week 9   Cycle 7 miles in twenty-one minutes, forty-five seconds
Week 10 Cycle 7 miles in twenty-one minutes, thirty seconds
Week 11 Cycle 7 miles in twenty-one minutes, fifteen seconds
Week 12 Cycle 7 miles in twenty-one minutes

Maintenance program for cycling is: Cycle 6 miles in twenty-one minutes, four times a week. Cycle 5 miles in fifteen to seventeen minutes, two times a week. Cycle 5 miles in twenty minutes once a week.

Walking—Beginning Level
Week 1   Walk 3/4 mile in twenty minutes, daily
Week 2   Walk 3/4 mile in seventeen minutes, thirty seconds, daily
Week 3   Walk 1 mile in twenty minutes, daily
Week 4   Walk 1 mile in nineteen minutes, thirty seconds, daily
Week 5   Walk 1 mile in nineteen minutes, daily
Week 6   Walk 1 mile in eighteen minutes, thirty seconds, daily
Week 7   Walk 1 mile in eighteen minutes, daily
Week 8   Walk 1 1/2 miles in twenty-seven minutes, daily
Week 9   Walk 1 3/4 miles in thirty-one minutes, thirty seconds, daily
Week 10 Walk 2 miles in thirty-six minutes, daily
Week 11 Walk 2 miles in thirty-five minutes, thirty seconds, daily
Week 12 Walk 2 miles in thirty-five minutes, daily

Walking—Intermediate Level
Week 1   Walk 2 miles in thirty-four minutes, thirty seconds
Week 2   Walk 2 miles in thirty-four minutes
Week 3   Walk 2 miles in thirty-three minutes, thirty seconds
Week 4   Walk 2 miles in thirty-three minutes
Week 5   Walk 2 miles in thirty-two minutes, thirty seconds
Week 6   Walk 2 miles in thirty-two minutes
Week 7   Walk 2 miles in thirty-one minutes, thirty seconds
Week 8   Walk 2 miles in thirty-one minutes
Week 9   Walk 2 miles in thirty minutes, forty-five seconds
Week 10   Walk 2 miles in thirty minutes, fifteen seconds
Week 11   Walk 2 miles in thirty minutes
Week 12   Walk 3 miles in forty-five minutes

Walking—Advanced Level
Week 1   Walk 3 miles in forty-four minutes, thirty seconds
Week 2   Walk 3 miles in forty-four minutes
Week 3   Walk 3 miles in forty-three minutes, thirty seconds
Week 4   Walk 3 miles in forty-three minutes
Week 5   Walk 3 miles in forty-two minutes, thirty seconds
Week 6   Walk 3 miles in forty-two minutes
Week 7   Walk 3 miles in forty-one minutes, thirty seconds
Week 8   Walk 3 miles in forty-one minutes
Week 9   Walk 3 miles in forty minutes, thirty seconds
Week 10   Walk 3 miles in forty minutes
Week 11   Walk 3 miles in thirty-nine minutes, thirty seconds
Week 12   Walk 3 miles in thirty-nine minutes

Maintenance program in walking: Walk 2 miles, four times a week, within twenty-four to twenty-six minutes. Walk 3 miles, twice a week, at thirty-six to thirty-seven minutes. Walk 1 mile once a week at fifteen minutes.

Heal Your Soul

DOCTORS OF PREVENTIVE medicine speak of nutritional detoxification and healing your mind and body as keys to lasting wellness. The eighth rule of High Performance Living takes your wellness program to the next level, because the focus is on how to heal your soul. Rejuvenating your soul is the winning strategy of this chapter.

Your soul is the spiritual part of your being. It is your spirit. In fact, it is spirit within your body. The seat of your soul is the center of your very essence. Your soul gives you the gift of life, and without a soul, there is no life as we know it. The light of your soul is the electricity that plugs you into life!

The light of your soul is the creative, life-giving energy vibrating and circulating within. The Chinese call it *Chi*, the Japanese call it *Qi*, the Indian yogis call it *Prana*. Your soul power focuses its attention on drawing out the light within your soul. With the light of your soul shining brightly, your heart naturally comes alive, and your mind gets lucid and clear. In fact, your soul power has the ability to heal your mind and your body.

The level of your soul power is revealed by your courage, determination, and morale. Your soul power gives you your strength and drive to experience the magnificence of spirit that is called fulfillment. Soul power is the inner wisdom that allows you to be happy, healthy, and free. Furthermore, your soul power gives you the zeal to find the light in your life.

Just as the power of your physical body needs quality nutrition to thrive, your soul needs to be well-nourished to grow and prosper. A healthy, well-nourished soul is the key to dynamic, invincible soul power. Enthusiasm, vigor, and passion are the vibrant greeting cards of the healthy soul. A tenacious commitment to happiness is the trademark of a healthy soul.

Heal Your Soul

Healing your soul simply said is living your life! It is an alliance with the true and real you. It is a fellowship with the convictions and secrets of your soul. It inspires you to be the best at what you instinctively and intuitively know the best—being yourself.

To heal your soul, you must satisfy your soul. You know you are doing a good job, because when you are healing your soul, you enjoy substantial peace of mind. You are serene and joyful. You are driven to improve yourself and fulfill your visions. You are prepared to get a grasp on your life and learn how to stay balanced in the yoga of life. Healing your soul is a process that teaches you to be reborn every day. It gets you in touch with your uniqueness and gives you the wisdom to seek out the truth in your life.

When you are restless, find it difficult to concentrate or stay focused on one thing at a time, you can do a better job at healing your soul. Spiritual fatigue can sometimes be difficult to diagnose. However, when you are easily distracted, confused, or anxious or feel that you are not doing what you want to be doing, you gradually become drained. Spiritual fatigue sets in, and you lose the will to love, the will to improve, and the will to live your life to the fullest.

Healing your soul ignites your thinking. Healing your soul enlivens your heart. It exerts a very positive influence on your immune body and puts a step in your walk. Healing your soul straightens out your posture. It gives character to your breath, puts boldness in your chest, and invites you to strut around taller and stronger, with your head held high. The strategies and techniques that empower you to heal your soul are divided into two major categories.

1) Nourishing Your Soul: feeding your soul what it needs.
2) Owning the Power of the Healing Consciousness: creating the proper inner-directed self-awareness to heal your soul.

A well-nourished soul creates a person who is playful, jubilant, cheerful, and animated. A well-nourished soul is absolutely essential for High Performance Living because it creates inner strength, balance, and calmness, while enhancing human efficiency. Peacefulness, gentleness, blissfulness, and tranquillity are the spiritual attributes of a well-nourished soul.

Soul Power Feeds Spiritual Well-Being

The fruits of optimal spiritual health are love, joy, creative self-expression, and inner peace. Being lively, bold, forceful, and glowing speaks well for a vital spirit. Later in this chapter, you will learn how meditation feeds your soul and how acquiring the healing consciousness energizes your soul power.

The opposite of a resilient spirit is a poorly nourished soul. Spiritual malnutrition is the end point of long-standing spiritual deficiencies caused by losing touch with yourself. Losing touch with your soul, and therefore yourself, is a root cause of burnout. This lack of harmony is usually due to a stressful overload of duties, deadlines, demands, responsibilities, and chores. Also, spiritual ignorance can result from an absence of spiritual guidance.

Spiritual malnutrition is characterized by a soul that has become suffocated and devitalized. As spiritual burnout builds up, spiritual sclerosis, or hardening of the spirit, develops. Much like atherosclerosis (hardening of the arteries) and psychosclerosis (hardening of the brain), the malnourished spirit becomes stiff and ossified. Everything is old or gets old fast. Nothing is new, and there is nothing to live for. Indifference and purposelessness can easily take over. Spiritual burnout is a common cause of mind dysfunction, emotional stress, and bodily decay.

Unless you keep your spirit pure and alive, your life goes downhill. In between spiritual burnout and spiritual well-being lies a twilight zone of spiritual mediocrity.

Spiritual
Well-Being
     Partial
     Spiritual
     Well-being
          Spiritual
          Mediocrity
               Spiritual
               Burnout
                    Spiritual
                    Malnutrition

When you are stuck in spiritual mediocrity, you are aware that there is something missing in life and there is more to life than what you are experiencing. Here, you get smart by finding out how much it smarts to be out of touch. Yet, you are not quite certain precisely what to do to get unstuck. By not fighting back against this creeping and confusing suffocation, your spiritual life begins to get covered up. In time, your soul gets suppressed enough to move into spiritual inertia. This invites depression and further darkens the light of your soul. When mediocrity turns into poor spiritual health (spiritual burnout), you become lost. You struggle to get by day by day without direction, rhyme, or reason. Even though your soul power is rapidly fading away, it is still not too late to do something about it. The difference between the vitality and enthusiasm of a healthy soul and the depression and listlessness of a burned out soul is in how well you nourish your soul.

How to Nourish Your Soul

Soul power is defined by a well-nourished soul. A well-nourished soul is essential to High Performance Living. There are ten essential nutrients to a well-nourished soul. These life-giving principles keep your spirits high. Taking care of yourself goes beyond eating well and exercising every day. Spiritual nutrition keeps your soul alive and well. Below are the ten nutrients that promote spiritual growth. Take inventory, and see how well your soul is fed. Also, determine what it would take for each nutrient to become a regular consistent support system in your life. Score: 5 for "Always" (daily), 4 for "Frequently" (usually), 3 for "Sometimes" (irregular), 2 for "Rarely," and 1 for "Never." Write in your choices and tally the points.

YOU:	Always	Usually	Sometimes	Rarely	Never
Stand up for what you believe in.	5	4	3	2	1
Have a purposeful balanced lifestyle.	5	4	3	2	1
Find creative self-expression regularly.	5	4	3	2	1
Spend time outdoors in nature being quiet, listening, and taking in your environment.	5	4	3	2	1
Communicate and spend time with loved ones.	5	4	3	2	1
Spend time in satisfying social and cultural activities.	5	4	3	2	1
Share laughter with kindred souls.	5	4	3	2	1
Eat well.	5	4	3	2	1
Exercise vigorously.	5	4	3	2	1
Spend quality time in devotional prayer and/or meditation at least one time a day, if not two to three times a day.	5	4	3	2	1

Total Points:

———————————

40–50 points	well-nourished soul
29–39 points	moderately nourished soul
19–28 points	poorly nourished soul

How Meditation Shapes Up Your Consciousness

Unless time is spent developing your inner life, it could easily be neglected. Meditation is an opportunity to communicate with your own heart and nourish your soul. It is a way to experience your higher loving self. Meditation is sustained concentration and devotion. Meditation empowers you to focus on your inner joy and inner feelings of bliss. This concentration on your heart and soul is the kind of harmony you need to experience your inner spirit and achieve self-awareness.

The idea in meditation is to calm your overactive mind. Unless you quiet your mind and break the endless distractions of your thinking, it is difficult to get through the static and experience love and peace within yourself. This is why meditation is so important for corporate executives, busy homemakers, and all highly stressed individuals.

Meditation relaxes you, empties your mind, and gets rid of the chaos and disorder in your thoughts. In effect, learn to get your mind out of the picture. In this way, you begin to touch base with your true feelings, your real self, and gain emotional reality testing. This kind of emotional intelligence can only be derived by acquiring inner wisdom, the very purpose of meditation.

The more sustained and concentrated your meditation, the more healing it becomes. The more your meditation gets you in touch with yourself, the more nourishing it is for your soul. Meditation is a tonic that has incredible benefits for the body. It has been scientifically documented to lower blood pressure, increase blood circulation, and effectively help the body reduce stress. It revitalizes your nerves and rejuvenates your hormones. It relaxes your body and purifies your emotions. It soothes your mind and cleanses your soul.

Like exercise and good nutrition, making meditation a daily habit is important. You could not exercise one day a week and consider yourself fit any more than you can meditate once in awhile and bring yourself into spiritual harmony. Most people are interested and open to learning about meditation, and everyone who practices it seems to feel that it helps them. The key is to inspire yourself to do it.

Why do some people meditate long-term and some people stop? For the same reasons that some people stay with a long-term nutritional program and fitness regime. They are committed to themselves, to High Performance Living, and to taking charge of their lives. They have embraced the discipline to be consistent when human nature is consistently inconsistent.

Meditation brings together prayer, ritual self-discipline, and celebration. There are three main types of meditation that you can learn to apply to heal your soul.

1) Mental Relaxation
2) Creative Imagination
3) Self-Healing

Mental relaxation. This kind of meditation gives you the opportunity to retreat from your daily stresses, struggles, and strain. Fix your mind on a peaceful, natural setting. For example, fix your attention on some green trees or beautiful flowers. Likewise, you can gaze at the waves or watch the setting sun. You can also listen to the waves at sea or the birds in the forest. Now then, shut off your thoughts, and let yourself go. Use deep cleansing breaths to slow down and calm your mind. Become one in mind, body, and spirit with your natural element. Let all tension drift away as you relax and feel yourself come alive. Stay with it for at least ten to fifteen minutes.

Creative imagination. This kind of meditation relies on the picture power of guided visual imagery. Here, you use your imagination to create the kind of events you want to be experiencing in your life. Visualize the circumstances at work, home, and play as you secretly desire. Direct the movie of your own mind to its wildest fantasy, and see yourself as the main interesting character. Be sure to not only see the experience, but more importantly, feel it, whether it is a vacation, adventure, or sexual interaction, as you like it. It is your creation. Practice this for ten to fifteen minutes to feel the full benefits.

Self-healing. Concentrating on the healing powers of your soul is the foundation to self-healing meditations. Affirmations investing and validating the power in your spirit are commonly used. Affirmations are statements of strong intent and belief repeated silently to yourself and then out loud. When repeated in a mantra-like (repetitive) fashion, they open up and interface a great deal of internal communication with your inner self. For example,

I am a pure channel of love and light.
My heart is alive with pure love and joy.
I have the power of Spirit to...
I believe in myself.

In the process of meditation, your soul naturally unfolds into its ultimate manifestation as a pure channel of love. Meditation purges the darkness of spiritual blindness, spiritual indigestion, and spiritual restlessness out of your life. Regular meditation enables you to find your heart center and live in the moment. By practicing meditation, it becomes an effortless spiritual instrument. Feel the love in your heart, listen to your inner voice, and you will discover the secrets of your soul. You will also touch base with the buried treasures in your heart.

How to Meditate

There are many different ways to meditate, from affirmations to Zen. Any technique that allows you full concentration on your heartfelt love and relaxation will get you into the Zone. This describes a state of being that results from becoming one with yourself. It empowers you to focus your undivided attention on healing from within. The ultimate meditation embraces a relaxed physical body, a pure loving heart, deep breathing, and a one-pointed, calm mind. Yoga and t'ai chi teach this very essence. For example, an effective meditation is sitting in a lotus position or assuming the t'ai chi horse stance. With your body in an effortless state, open your heart, gently gaze upwards, and practice deep cleansing breaths, one at a time. Put a smile in your heart, your soul, and your eyes. This will recharge your spirit.

In general, please review the following eight essential steps that lead to effective in-depth meditation. This eclectic technique will teach you how to meditate and heal your soul.

Step 1   Relax your physical body (precede meditation with exercise, yoga, or t'ai chi).

Step 2   Sit up straight, keep your spine straight and head upright. Get ready to look within, quiet the mind, and focus on your spirit.

Step 3   Practice deep cleansing breaths using a rhythm of 2:4:4:2 (inhale for two, hold for four, exhale for four counts, then hold for two). Work up to 4:8:8:4. Concentrate and listen to your breath. Breathe loud enough so that someone walking by would hear it.

Step 4   Heartfelt meditation is the key. With every breath, fill your heart with love. Allow your heart space to expand. Feel the bliss and the unconditional love for yourself and others. You choose how you feel. Focus within on the light of your soul.

Step 5   Expand your heart space, and calm your mind. With love from your heart, concentrate on your "third eye" (the central point between your eyebrows). With your eyes closed, allow an upward gaze, and look within. Be sure to relax the eye muscles in the front and back of your eye.

Step 6   Focus on healing affirmations that are strong feelings of purpose, conviction, belief, and self-acceptance. Affirmations open your heart and heal your soul. Use these affirmations or make up your own:

- I believe in myself.
- I love life.
- My faith will make me whole.
- I expect to be happy.
- Heal my mind, heal my body, heal my heart, and heal my soul.
- The power of creation loves me!

Step 7   Creative Visualizations—See your dreams come true before you. Guide your imagination to visualize an optimal situation, lifestyle, or circumstance.

Step 8   Relax, let go, and flow with inner joy and peace. Transcend your busy mind, and bliss out!

The Healing Consciousness Balances Out Your Spiritual Life

In healing your soul and keeping your spirits high, the key is to move your soul into a consciousness of healing. The healing consciousness is necessary to develop your soul power. The healing consciousness is the dynamic state of heightened emotional awareness and spiritual sensitivity. A healing consciousness uplifts your perceptions, thoughts, feelings, and experiences to the infinite boundaries of heartfelt love, emotional fulfillment, and spiritual prosperity.

It is your level of consciousness that determines your quality of life. Your consciousness is your experience. It is common to choose a level of consciousness that sets you up to be rich in possessions but poor in spirit, poor in health, and emotionally bankrupt. In actuality, there are five different levels of consciousness.

Survival consciousness. This level of consciousness sets in when your awareness is dominated by survival. To Robert, a thirty-four-year-old salesman, living was having a job and just getting by. Some people go through life making things happen. Robert went through life saying, "what happened?" He did not prioritize the quality of his life.

When you are immersed in survival consciousness, you see life as a struggle to exist. Robert was either worried about how to maintain a financial position for the future or fearful of losing what he had accomplished. He was existing, not living. He was looking for security from his external world instead of within. After all, when a pickpocket sees a saint, all he sees is his pockets.

Sex consciousness. Preoccupation with your own sexual needs, sexual fantasies, and addiction to your sexual fulfillment are the main symptoms of being dominated by sex consciousness. Here, sex is always on the brain, and your thinking and emotions are determined by your sex drive.

For Marty, a thirty-five-year-old attorney, his sexual instincts and hunting down his animalistic nature were the predominant features of his personality. His lifestyle, clothing, mannerisms, and expressions were designed to enhance his sex appeal. Marty was convinced that to be happy, all he needed was the right sexual partner. In spite of many lovers, he could never get enough. He was forever frustrated and disappointed.

The lack of sexual fulfillment can be a source of ongoing distractions. Although sexual fulfillment is crucial to realizing your total potential and fulfillment, it can easily become an emotional addiction. When you integrate your emotional life and your sexual life, sexual fulfillment becomes a stepping stone to greater emotional gratification. When sex and love are in harmony, it is healing to your heart and soul.

Power consciousness. Engrossed with being in control rather than being controlled; the consciousness of power becomes a way of life. It is popular among those codependents and counterdependents who need to exercise control over others.

Joann had worked her way up to becoming vice president at a real estate firm. She enjoyed telling others what to do. She had lots of competition but fell victim to the old adage, "Power corrupts." Power consciousness is usually all-encompassing. Once you attain the power, it is easy to become addicted to keeping the power.

Joann's power consciousness became a trap. Her lustful addiction for more and more power got her stuck in a vicious cycle that took over her life. Her communication skills at work were great. At home, her relationships with her husband and children were falling apart, while her health was faltering. She worshiped the consciousness of power and lost touch with the power in her personal life.

Material consciousness. Success is often measured in our culture more by material worth than a person's true worth as an enriched, kind, enlightened, whole human being. When you become preoccupied with your possessions and material values, the commercialized material consciousness of the working world owns you.

Andy was a well-to-do financier. At age twenty-nine, he was already a baron on Wall Street, consumed with keeping his investments growing. He was always making lots of money and spent much of his free time planning tax shelters for it. He was compulsively driven to being a multimillionaire. What he did not realize was that the more successful he was becoming on the outside, the more hollow he was becoming on the inside. He forfeited his family and personal relationships at the expense of his work. He thrived on competition and putting his opponents in their place.

Survival, sexual fulfillment, accomplishment, and material reinforcement are fundamental realities in modern living. However, by themselves, they do not breed excellent health or lasting happiness. There is more to life than sex, money, power, and success. For permanent well-being, the winning strategy is to own the power of the healing consciousness.

Healing consciousness. The healing consciousness awakens the healing vibrations of your soul. It heals the heartaches of your soul, while it purges negative thoughts and feelings within. Keep in mind that your true level of healing your soul and your level of consciousness are inseparable. This is the truth of the healing sciences. Healing and consciousness have a mind/body relationship. It is only with the attitude and foundation of a healing consciousness, in conjunction with the right foods, appropriate exercise, and a balanced lifestyle, that you can achieve High Performance Living.

Pay Respect to Divine Light and Pure Love

The healing consciousness purifies your soul. The pure soul is a clear channel of light and love. In the most symbolic of terms then, the healing consciousness is a state of being, dominated by divine light and pure love.

The match that lights the fire of the healing consciousness is the creative inspirational love energy in your heart. This pure love turns out to be the magical key that opens the door to the secrets of your all-knowing soul. Consistently feeling heartfelt love, thinking positively, and gaining creative insight into yourself is the proof that you are experiencing the healing consciousness.

Your level of heartfelt love is the catalyst to your spiritual awakening. It is only through your ongoing expansion of heartfelt love that your soul can eventually ascend the different levels of consciousness and become spiritually awakened to healing your soul. You see, in the light of the soul, there are only two emotions: Love for life or fear of inadequacy.

The healing consciousness is your inner wisdom manifested. This inner wisdom unfolds from heartfelt harmony with the divine light and pure love within. Soul wisdom arouses your soul power.

The Triangle of the Healing Consciousness

There are three spiritual muscles—love, faith, and peace of mind—that need daily exercise to develop the triangle of a healing consciousness.

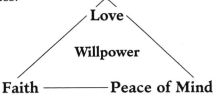

Faith in spirit, heartfelt love, and peace of mind come together to enrich your soul power. Your willpower drives your spiritual muscles.

Faith

Faith is the willingness to believe in the fulfillment of your dreams. Faith is knowing that you can grow in all circumstances to make your life work out for the best. It is a total belief that you have the inner power to be whole and happy. No matter what the predicament, you will find the inner strength to see things to a favorable resolution.

The healing consciousness is sustained by a calm, loving, hopeful, faithful spirit. Faith is the union of belief, trust, and spiritual conviction. It grounds your soul to the possibility of miracles. Faith steers you through the storms of your life. It brings oxygen to the spirit, and without the oxygen, the fire of the spirit has no flame.

When you have the faith, you are comfortable in emotionally surrendering your deepest spiritual convictions to the higher order of the universe. Faith is born out of complete yielding to the will of the Spirit. Faith in the love and in the light of your soul is not only fundamental to having "the faith" but also is the key to opening the magic door of the healing consciousness.

When you move forward in life with a strong active belief in yourself and in the light, you are on the path to having faith. Strong characters of faith know the more you experience the faith, the more you will experience the healing consciousness.

You Need to Have the Faith

Develop the faith to overcome any dilemma by discovering the soul power in your faith. This will cause your faith to grow and grow. Start with small predicaments, and see how faith has a powerful organizing influence on your mind. Artistically build your bridge of faith from some simple disciplines that follow.

- Find a natural setting to meditate. Skillfully relax your body and mind. Sit up straight, and breathe deeply until you feel your heart center.
- Warm up to the faith by asking yourself what blessings in life you have to be thankful for? Relax and let go even further.
- Imagine yourself in a room where you are surrounded by a warm bright halo of light like sunlight. Inhale the light, and as you bring the warmth and light into your body, feel the faith expanding within your body. As you inhale, ask yourself what in your life needs healing? Then listen! The key is to listen to yourself and the intuitive wisdom of your inner voice.
- Be patient, and await your answers. Then ask yourself, what specific actions can you take to affect this healing? Then, move forward with your strong and active faith.
- Keep the faith through thick and thin. Keep breathing into your expanding balloon until you feel swollen inside with the faith of the healing consciousness. Keep in mind that faith is food to your soul, just as love is nutrition to your heart. Practice this exercise so you may recruit the faith to resolve conflicts.

Stand by Your Faith

With your faith guiding you, search yourself on the grounds of what you spiritually believe in. This is the foundation for your spiritual commitments. Believe in the infinite healing power of your heartfelt love. Stand up for yourself, your loved ones, and the light. Make a commitment to the real expression of the light in your soul and the love in your heart.

Another meditation technique for developing faith is to repeat over and over the affirmation, "my faith will make me whole." Remember, with practice, discipline, repetition, and focus, you can learn to use your faith to heal your soul and keep your spirits high. Try to believe that no matter what the predicament, you can find the inner strength to see it through to a favorable conclusion. Now then, answer the following question:

What kind of things can you do to build your faith?

Turn on Your Love

The next spiritual muscle in cultivating the healing consciousness is heartfelt love. Love is the most powerful healing force in the universe. Your love can make you whole. The deeper the level of love in your life, the more meaning and fullness to your life. With love in your heart and courage to back you up, realize that anything is possible: no task is to great, no adventure or dream an impossibility. You know you are experiencing the healing consciousness when you feel pure love and joy in your heart. It is there for you to embrace at all times.

Be Rich in Love

You have the choice to experience love or fear as the dominant emotion in your life. When you are fully attuned to being happy, do any negative attitudes or beliefs exist? Of course not! How rich your life is can be measured by the kinds and amounts of love in your life. From the inner reservoir of your love grows strength and compassion. Love and faith open the gates to divine bliss!

How do you become rich in love? The more love you radiate, the more you will get back. Think back to what truly turns you on. Do you give yourself permission to feel the penetrating warmth of all powerful joy? Real love is spontaneous, natural, and effortless. Attune yourself to its flow.

To enhance the feelings of heartfelt love, go back to the most basic primary love experience you know. Whatever it is, while you are doing it:

- Turn your attention on to your heart. Feel the soft, beautiful warmth within your chest. Experience total bliss.
- Affirm softly with each inhalation, "My heart is alive." After a deep inhalation and a pause, enjoy the breathless state. Then with expiration, say, "with pure love and joy."
- Therefore, "My heart is alive" (inspiration) "with pure love and joy" (expiration) will enable you to feel the expansion in your heart. Repeat this affirmation for five minutes. Then bliss out.

Loving people are happy people, and those who feel the most love are the happiest people of all. At the end of each day, be sure to ask yourself: "How much love did I generate today for the people that came into my life?" How often do you tell people in your life, "I love you"? Feel yourself pregnant with love. This is an important technique for developing love in your heart to heal your soul. Expand your love relationships. Carry this love with you everywhere you go. Become a channel of love. Love and faith open the gates of the healing consciousness.

What can you do to feel more love and make those you care about feel more loved and appreciated?

Mind Your Peace

Peace of mind is the third vital component in creating a consciousness of healing. With love in your heart, faith in your spirit, and peace in your mind, the healing consciousness creates a sound and strong equilateral triangle of support to healing your soul.

No one but yourself can bring inner peace to your life. Lasting, real peace of mind comes from an alliance with your higher loving self. This inner peace begets creativity, productivity, and sound decision making. Peace of mind is a soothing tonic for your soul. Real peace of mind results from being at ease with who you are and at one with what you are doing with your life.

Shangri-la Can Be Yours

Practice this simple Shangri-la exercise whenever you are restless, uptight, upset, or out of touch.

- Close your eyes, relax, and tune into the love in your heart. Feel great, and then center yourself by attuning to the light in your soul.
- Climb a flight of storybook stairs to one of your favorite vacation retreats. Feel the exhilaration of being where you want to be.
- Create a Shangri-la environment with your imagination. Use your vivid mind to embellish your favorite retreat with all the circumstances and details of how you would like to spend your time. Recruit birds singing, the wind whistling. Consider the kind of people you would have there with you. Imagine having the most fulfilling love relationships. Hold this vision, and feel this experience.
- Now let yourself go. Become the happy star or starlet of your own movie. You are the hero or heroine in Shangri-la. Camera, action, roll 'em. The scene is set. Spend

fifteen minutes enjoying this movie. Take this peace and calmness of Shangri-la with you wherever you go.

What action steps can you take to create more peace of mind?

Focus Your Willpower

At the center of your healing triangle is your willpower. A strong spiritual will is necessary to pierce the darkness in your life to see the inner light and to penetrate the loving vibrations in your heart. You need your willpower to keep your focus on healing your soul. You know you are drinking the nectar of the healing consciousness when you experience more love, joy, and peace every day. Staying focused on the love in your heart and the light of your soul transforms you into a new level of healing. In this transformation, you own the power of the healing consciousness. Your heartfelt love combined with your soul wisdom and joyful inner peace fires up your spirit and heals your soul.

To be rich in spirit and to keep your spirits high, nourishing your soul is the preferred technique. Through the effective habit of meditation, you can nourish your soul and convert this well-being into a healing consciousness. This will develop your soul power, faith, love, and peace of mind. Stand up for what you believe, and watch your spirit grow. Watch it soar like an eagle flying high in the sky. Keep the faith, be peaceful, and above all, experience the love and light in your soul.

Define Your Purpose in Life

THE NINTH RULE of High Performance Living is "Define Your Purpose in Life." Your purpose in life is your direction in life. It is your cause, your message, your objective. A happy, healthy soul needs a meaningful, purposeful life. The purpose in your life touches your heart and activates your soul to come alive.

Your purpose is your identity. Simply said, it is what means the most to you. Have you found your purpose in life? Your purpose in life feeds your spiritual health and is a stepping stone to long-standing happiness. When you are in optimal spiritual health, it is a given that you stand by and hold true to your purpose in life. Your purpose is the invisible cement that keeps your ambition in harmony with your destiny. It is the target of your intentions and in time gives you spiritual freedom. Your purpose is your endless determination to find your place in the sun. In time, it becomes the ceaseless commitment to your happiness and the prophecy of your soul.

You own the key to the mystery of finding the purpose in your life. We all have different purposes for the varying stages in our lives. In the early years, from birth to eighteen or so, you play and go to school. You really do not have to take life that seriously during this time. Those who do usually suffer from over-maturity. They spend the rest of their life trying to have a good time and recapture their lost adolescence. However, as you approach college age, your purpose becomes to get an education and learn how to live on your own. After college, it is typical to search for your financial and emotional independence. Your purpose in life then turns toward your career, your security, and the challenges of finding your soul mate and starting your family. Then, from your early thirties onward, you face the challenges of staying in harmony with your purpose in life. This is no simple matter since your purpose in life changes in accordance with how your values change.

Look today at the common life crises of teenagers, college graduates, people turning thirty or forty, midlifers, menopausal women, divorcees, or career changers. These crises center on one common thread. People are reevaluating the direction or purpose in their life. They are saying to themselves, "There has to be more to life than this." Well, I am here to assure you that there is.

When you have purpose, you naturally feel good about yourself. Purposeful living is conducive to inner peace and joy. Just as the mind needs to think positively, the heart needs to love, and the body needs exercise; the soul needs purpose!

Just as purposeful living nourishes the soul, the opposite also rings true. A lack of purpose is very stressful and creates restlessness and self-damaging anxiety. Purposelessness is a state of spiritual deficiency. It weakens the immune system and essentially increases your vulnerability to illness. When you lack purpose, you feel trapped. Your soul suffocates and begins to burn out. A lack of purpose hardens the soul and increases the risk of degenerative illnesses like cancer, stroke, heart disease, and arthritis. This is most clearly seen in successful male executives who within two years after retirement are either dead, severely depressed, or suffering with a serious disease. What happened? These people had purpose with their work. Once their work ended, they lost their purpose in life. Purpose in life is a need of the spirit. Without purpose, the light of the soul begins to fade and extinguish the flame of life.

Nick Finds Out

I remember Nick when we first met at a health convention in San Diego in 1971. He had a youthful, pleasant appearance. He was tall, clear-skinned, had a firm handshake, and did not look like the fifty years he carried.

Nick was an intelligent, composed individual and presented himself to others as a happy-go-lucky entrepreneur. However, underneath his mask, he was introverted and frightened. In the last two years, he suffered with progressive weakness and fatigue that worsened as the day went on. "Doctor, I feel that everything is falling apart. I tire easily, and I've lost my get up and go. By 4:00 in the afternoon, I'm beat. I feel like there's something wrong with me, but I don't know what it is; neither does my internist. He can find nothing wrong with me. I used to play a lot of tennis, dance, ski, and play volleyball. Now, I'm too wiped out at the end of the day to be doing any kind of exercise. Each day it seems like life is becoming a little more work and a little less fun. I see myself as mounting inner tensions. I can't stick to one thing, even when I think I want to do it. Like I'll show an interest in a new class, and before I know it, I've dropped it. What's wrong with me Doc? I'm not mixing well with other people, and I have lost my entire sex drive.

In searching into his background, I learned that Nick's life had become empty. His daughters had grown up and left home.

He had become bored with running his restaurant business. Last year, he and his wife Carla took separate vacations. Nick went to Mexico, and Carla went to the Philippines. He did not like it and came home after one week. Carla never came back. She wrote that she was not in the best of health and was teaching bible classes at an English language school.

Nick's personal life was devoid of any love. He was withdrawing from life. I told Nick that he was suffering with severe depression. The cause of his negative emotional state was that he did not have any real meaning or purpose in his life. I asked Nick what his purpose in life was. He shared that he had no idea and did not know what he wanted to do. His family had left him. His ex-wife had died from breast cancer while overseas. His parents were no longer alive. His children had grown and left home. I told Nick that there was a cure for this common spiritual deficiency called purposelessness, "Purpose in your life is an emotional salve that can soothe your ailing soul. Pay attention to your soul, and you can get well. Ignore your soul, and you will live in hell. The purpose in life is to be happy. The purpose in your life is to experience the world of happiness within you."

When you are not in touch with your purpose in life, there is a breakdown in your internal communication. This causes you an energy drain. Long-standing purposelessness creates fatigue and weakness. It is at the root of many biochemical, emotional, and psychological imbalances.

I told Nick that to find himself, he would need to spend in-depth time in meditation with nature. I asked him to answer the following questions:

- How do you want to spend the rest of your life?
- What is it in life that you most want to experience?
- What contribution do you want to make to your fellow humans?

- Where do you feel you belong and with whom?
- How do you see yourself in your wildest fantasies?

Through a regular meditation program, Nick was able to get in touch with his own uniqueness. I explained to him that regular periods of quiet self-realization would reveal the secrets of his soul.

"Nick, the purpose in life, simply said, is to be yourself. The purpose of life is to love and be loved. Your undaunted commitment to your unique purpose is the basis for your self-esteem. Having purpose in your life is to experience the infinite healing and loving potential within you. Once you get clear as to your purpose in life, it is a simple matter to set up the strategies to realize your purpose."

Nick became a dedicated student of the Ten Rules of High Performance Living. He started jogging daily, cleaned up his diet, did yoga every morning, and got tuned into his own healing consciousness. He began to look upon his weakness, fatigue, and depression as an opportunity to be reborn. Within six weeks of regular meditation, he made a breakthrough in his thinking. He had always wanted to open a bed and breakfast weekend retreat in the mountains of northern Oregon. He started saving his money for this. He began to spend more time hiking and camping in nature. He realized that his happiness came from within. He found purpose to his life that touched his heart and empowered his soul. Nine months later, he was becoming well-adjusted and living a high performance lifestyle.

When people are happy, healthy, and feeling good about themselves, they have purpose. You know you have purpose when you are strong, fit, upbeat, and spirited. When you are purposeful, you are making a contribution to others, expressing yourself, and adhering to a life of self-enrichment. As long as you are breathing, you have a purpose in life. Lack of purpose in life is really a mirage. Purposelessness, in fact, is an escape. It is convenient to say you have no purpose because it often represents the path of least resistance.

The fact is we all have a purpose in life. You are endowed with a unique purpose with special qualities and individual features to develop this purpose. You and I and every living soul on this planet have a special mission in this lifetime.

You Are the Captain of Your Soul

In looking for purpose, once again, it is totally up to you. It is your responsibility to know yourself and get in touch with your heart and soul. Only you know what means the most to you. Everyone has the privilege to validate their mission and develop their unique qualities.

We Have More Than One Purpose

Our purpose in life is multidimensional. Your mind, body, spirit, and heart each have purpose. You also have purpose in your connection with loved ones, family, and friends. You can also have a purpose in relationship to your career.

There are a number of different ways to look at your purpose in life. You can find purpose in life spiritually, emotionally, mentally, and physically. Purposeful living is defined as being the best at being yourself. You can find purpose in being needed, in being useful, and enriching the lives of others. You can also say that the purpose in life is to be happy, healthy, and free. The key is that when you pursue whatever it takes to be happy, healthy, and free, you will naturally come to terms with your purpose in life. Why? Because without being in touch with your purpose, you cannot sustain being happy, healthy, and free.

How to Find Your Purpose in Life

The following questions will help you get comfortable with finding your purpose in life. Find an inspiring, tranquil setting, and with pencil and paper in hand, answer these questions.

What is missing in your life?

What means more to you than anything else in your life?

In what area of life do you want to make a difference, more than any other?

What, more than anything else, do you want to do with your precious life?

How would you prefer to spend the majority of your time?

Do you wake up each morning with love in your heart, enthusiastic and excited about a new day? If not, why?

When you have purpose, you are excited and ready to move. Sometimes, you have to get past thinking about duties, obligations, and responsibilities to get to know your purpose. For example, use the following questions to gain insight that can be supportive in your search.

If you were a millionaire and money was no object, how would you spend your time?

How would you spend the next six to nine months if you were told you only had that much longer to live?

What do you live for?

What is your cause?

What are you trying to get people to understand?

Finding your purpose in life is manifested through the experience of getting to know your higher loving self. Through a regular, consistent, in-depth meditation program, you can become tuned into your inner wisdom and find your purpose. Creative, soulful introspection is the guiding strategy that will give you your answers. It will enable you to find the kingdom of God-consciousness within you. Use the following formula to find your purpose in life.

- Spend time alone in a quiet, tranquil, natural, outdoor setting (for example: listen to the crashing waves, birds in the morning sun, the penetrating rhythm of a mountain stream).
- Feel the bliss in your heart, quiet your mind, and find the secrets of your soul. Ten deep cleansing breaths will enable you to let your mental barriers down and let go.
- Focus on what you are feeling; turn off your mind and your thinking. Listen to your breathing. Feel and experience inner silence.
- Recognize your inner essence, and acknowledge the uniqueness of your very own self. Fully accept who you are, and appreciate and love yourself.
- Look within, and see yourself meeting up with a wise sage in your natural setting. Ask him or her, "What is my cause? What do I most strongly believe in? What is my purpose in life?"
- Wait for the answer. Keep repeating this exercise daily until the answer is revealed.

Now then, make three separate columns for each different purpose you discover. In the first column, list your purpose. In the second column, note any obstacles to this purpose. In the third column, determine the action steps necessary to make this purpose a reality. Follow the examples in the columns on the following page for this exercise:

Purpose	Obstacles (Examples)	Action Steps
1) find true love in my life	negative thinking	take charge of my attitude and beliefs
2) teach English to learning disabled	trapped at present job	get new credentials
3) heal my body	digestive troubles	change my diet, reduce my stress

Your Purposes

Passion Leads to Purpose

Another major technique for determining your purpose in life is to find out what really turns you on. In other words, be true to the passions in your life. Rekindling your passion for life is a certain bet to give you purpose. In pursuing your passions in life, you will bring your purpose into clear focus.

Do not allow anything to stop you from being happy, joyful, and purposeful. Take some time to answer the questions in this look-within quiz. This will help you find out what turns you on. Then, after you get impregnated with your passions, go for it! Honoring and pursuing the passion in your life will bring purpose to your life.

Dr. Barnet's "Look Within" Quiz

1) My joys in life are _____.
2) I love to _____.
3) _____
   turns me on.
4) I find _____
   to be the most exciting thing in my life.
5) The thrill of my life is _____.
6) I enjoy being alone and _____.
7) The secret, untold fantasies in my life are _____
   _____.
8) I find _____
   more interesting than anything in my life.
9) My greatest fascination in life is _____.
10) The most fun things in my life are _____.
11) The kinds of things I want to do with my life and have
    not yet done are _____.
12) _____
    will give me more freedom in my life.
13) To be happy, I need _____
    in my life.
14) More than anything else, I care about _____.
15) I have the strongest belief in _____
    in my life.

16) I find joy in my heart when _____.
17) I want to take an adventure to _____.
18) _____
     makes me feel really good inside.
19) _____
     takes me to the limit.
20) My emotions are aroused by _____.
21) _____
     inspires me to live each day to the fullest.
22) I would like to do _____
     that nobody else has ever done.
23) The inconsistencies I am perplexed by are _____
     _____.
24) I cannot stand _____.
25) In my free time, I like to _____.

Turning on to the passion, joy, and love in your life transforms the mystery of your life into the miracle of your life. These simple revelations of what turns you on triggers creative self-expression. This gives you the strength of character you have been looking for. What a great feeling! Pursue your passions, and it will give you purpose. This natural process opens the door to emotionally come alive.

Your Sex Life Counts

The final aspects of purposeful living that need to be addressed are the sensuality and sexuality issues in your life. Individuals need to be sexually fulfilled to be healthy and whole. Each person needs to figure out for themselves what they need to be sexually fulfilled. It is your sex life, just like it is your attitude, your belief system, your diet, and your day. You and your significant other will find that when you have purpose in your love life and sex life, you will be healthier and happier. The full realization of your sensuality and your optimal physical well-being are the fruit of the relationship tree. They go together like love and marriage.

Sexual enthusiasm perks up your energy level. There is wonder in everything you see. The excitement of your sex life brings your heart to life. You do not need as much sleep, your eating habits come under control, and your mind centers more easily when you are sexually fulfilled. Your attitudes about sex and the way you manifest your sensuality are distinctive features of your personality. Let it be emphasized that your love life and the health of your whole being are inseparable. Intimate sexual harmony with your lover touches your soul. A moonlit night of sweet love intoxicates you with the zest for life.

Let's be real. Our society places a high premium on being sexually attractive. The cosmetic and entertainment industries, the clothing stores, hair styling boutiques, and sports car promotional materials have one thing in common. They are appealing to your sex appeal. Sexual interactions in daytime soap operas, million dollar movies, TV advertisements, popular books, and magazine covers capitalize on your interest in sex.

Wherever you turn, attractive, voluptuous female models display pen and pencil sets, Jacuzzis, and automobiles. The media has you believing that when you lose your midriff bulge and cure your baldness, you will be certain to have a well-endowed gorgeous woman at your side. On Sunday afternoon, sexy cheerleaders entertain you on the sidelines. It is enough to drive even the most sane, crazy. Big business knows that people have a genuine interest in their sex lives. Sexy promotions cash in and make for greater profits.

Macho he-men hunks are the male sex symbols. They bring out the pure darkness in all of us. Their movies sell. Vital, firm feeling, titillating women become the sexual goddesses. They flood the media, one more beautiful than the last. The truth is that sex is here to stay. Indeed, your sexuality is a very creative form of needed self-expression. It is most nourished through the give and take of cherished interpersonal love relationships.

Keep in mind that your sexual personality is an intimate means to sharing your love. Your sensuality allows you to show others how you feel about them. Your sensuality gives you an opportunity to acknowledge the most special people in your life. Everybody thrives on acknowledgment from loved ones, and your sex life gives you the chance to appreciate your lover. Whether you run a high or low sexual profile, your sensuality and sexuality add punch to the purpose of your life. What you as an individual need to feel turned on and fully alive will guide you in your interpersonal relationships.

Find the mission and passion in your life, and you will know your purpose. Honor yourself and your true feelings. Take your purpose to the next level. What will it take to get you inspired?

In speaking to a spiritual master, one may say that your purpose in life is to become self-realized and to know the depths of your blissful and peaceful soul. It can be argued that your purpose in life is to be reborn everyday, to be fresh, alive, and totally be yourself. Others might reason that your purpose in life is to grow up in your first twenty-five years, raise your family and dedicate to your career from twenty-five to fifty, and thereafter, find enlightenment. Some others might argue that your purpose is to die well with a smile on your face. Whatever you discover, a conscious commitment to your purpose in life will lead you to High Performance Living.

When you are prepared to pay any price, bear any burden, and willing to meet any hardship to be true to your purpose, you are playing the game of life to win and are a seasoned player in High Performance Living. Remember, point yourself in the direction of what turns you on and what feels right for you. Stand up for what you believe. Find the passion in your life, and kindle its fire in the seat of your soul. Creatively express yourself, your sensuality, and your sexuality, and you will be in stride and on target. With purpose, you will experience emotional infinity in your spiritual timelessness.

With these points in mind, what is your purpose in life?

Balance Your Lifestyle

"BALANCE YOUR LIFESTYLE" is the tenth rule of High Performance Living. Your lifestyle is the way you choose to live your life. It is your relationship with how you spend your time. Your values, priorities, beliefs, attitudes, creativity, personal resources, consciousness, and financial status determine the character of your lifestyle. It is a direct reflection of who you are. The way you spend your time is the manifestation of how you see life. In essence, it is your most obvious form of self-expression.

Your lifestyle is a measure of your pace of living. A balanced, meaningful lifestyle is most conducive to wellness and ongoing high performance. The benefit of a balanced lifestyle is that it nourishes your whole being: your mind, your body, your emotions, your spirit. Your mind needs to think positively, your emotions need to manifest love, your spirit needs to find purpose, and your body needs fitness. A balanced lifestyle addresses your needs at all these levels.

Today, we live in a time of rapid change, inflationary stress, and cultural extremism. Traditional values are no longer above being questioned, reevaluated, and modified. The Protestant work ethic has been challenged, yet workaholism and alcoholism are rampant. Male/Female roles are changing. The nuclear family is struggling for its life. Increasing numbers of children are being raised by single parents. A minority of the people have the majority of the money. The rich get richer, and the poor grow poorer.

High density lifestyles are putting pressure on an unpredictable economy. Women are prioritizing their careers and are opting toward having children later in life with smaller families. Successful male executives are paying a dear price for their financial independence with burnout, bad health, substance abuse, impotence and broken down relationships. Our natural resources are being threatened with air, water, soil, and food pollution. As we approach the new millennium, we are suffering with mounting ecological and emotional stress. Finding balance in your life is becoming nearly un-American, and your lifestyle invariably reflects imbalances that derive from a confused and emotionally deprived culture. So how are we supposed to find balance when most of us are trapped in our own imbalances?

It is important to realize that things can change! You can learn and grow from your past experiences. Your lifestyle, in actuality, is an opportunity to change the course of your life. It is your responsibility to make the appropriate adjustments to create a balanced lifestyle. You will have to get back to the basics of the Ten Rules of High Performance Living. "Simplify," "lighten up," and "take charge of your life" are the foundation to balancing your lifestyle.

Your Inner Lifestyle Counts

Above all, remember that what is going on within you and the process of *how you do what you are doing* have the greatest impact on your everyday life. In other words, whether you choose to have fun and stay calm within throughout your day influences the journey in pursuit of its destination. A balanced lifestyle is truly a life where you are at one with yourself as well as in harmony with your environment. When your behavior is dominated by stress, fear, and anxiety, it is unlikely that you are in balance.

To acquire a balanced lifestyle, you will need training, discipline, patience, and tools. These are the steps you must climb to create balance:

- Take charge of your life, and take command of how you spend your time.
- Take the full responsibility for creating and experiencing a lifestyle of wellness.
- Make the effort to fully commit to a balanced lifestyle everyday.
- Be honest with yourself.

You can begin by getting familiar with your very own lifestyle. Answer these questions, and get in touch with what is really going on. You will need to know the strengths and weaknesses that prevail in order to fine tune yourself into daily balance.

How many hours a day do you spend playing or having fun?

How much time do you spend at work? Do you have a work-related lifestyle?

How much time do you spend at home with your family, loved ones, or friends?

How much time do you devote each day to personal growth?

How much time do you budget each day for keeping yourself healthy and prioritizing your self-care with fitness?

personal hygiene?

meditation?

relaxation?

Take Inventory

Sizing up the personality of your lifestyle is necessary for you to understand how you spend your time. Every day there needs to be time for personal growth, primary love relationships, social life, fun, career, work, eating, sleeping, household chores and duties, personal grooming, recreational activities, personal business, hobbies, and passive entertainment (TV, radio, reading). Since there is so much to integrate into a balanced lifestyle, let's start by thinking about identifying the details and important aspects of your own lifestyle. As you gain understanding into what kind of lifestyle you are buying into, you will be prepared to follow the lessons in this chapter. Establish a more meaningful balanced lifestyle, and enrich the quality of your life.

Sizing Up the Personality of Your Lifestyle

Determine from 1–10 where you stand in the personality of your lifestyle. Next to each component, commit to the action steps needed to improve your lifestyle.

Is/Does Your Lifestyle		*Preference/Action Steps*
idle, sedentary	1 2 3 4 5 6 7 8 9 10	physically invigorating
emotionally draining	1 2 3 4 5 6 7 8 9 10	emotionally energizing
lower your spirits	1 2 3 4 5 6 7 8 9 10	lift your spirits
conducive to indoors	1 2 3 4 5 6 7 8 9 10	conducive to outdoors
with difficulty nourish mind, body, spirit, emotion	1 2 3 4 5 6 7 8 9 10	easily nourish mind, body, spirit, emotion
no time to do what you want	1 2 3 4 5 6 7 8 9 10	time to do what you want
no time for deep breath and appreciation of surroundings	1 2 3 4 5 6 7 8 9 10	time for deep breath and appreciation of surroundings
dull, boring	1 2 3 4 5 6 7 8 9 10	interesting

Is/Does Your Lifestyle		*Preference/Action Steps*
synthetic	1 2 3 4 5 6 7 8 9 10	natural
random	1 2 3 4 5 6 7 8 9 10	organized
status quo	1 2 3 4 5 6 7 8 9 10	quality oriented
passive	1 2 3 4 5 6 7 8 9 10	assertive
dependent on environment	1 2 3 4 5 6 7 8 9 10	independent
aggravating	1 2 3 4 5 6 7 8 9 10	delightful
monotonous	1 2 3 4 5 6 7 8 9 10	creative
stressful	1 2 3 4 5 6 7 8 9 10	relaxed
narrow-minded	1 2 3 4 5 6 7 8 9 10	open-minded
purposeless	1 2 3 4 5 6 7 8 9 10	meaningful

Total Points:

_____

Less than 9 means you can make time for adjustments.

Compare the responses of your current lifestyle with your desired responses. Write out what specifically stands in your way for each one of these desired dimensions to be realized. Decide what action you can start doing today to make a change. It is the habit of finding solutions and thinking positively in the face of our predicaments that makes all the difference. The facts are clear. You choose your lifestyle, just as you choose your friends. You can become master of your lifestyle. It can serve to nourish your whole being. It is totally up to you.

Design an Optimal Lifestyle

How much you value your own self-worth, your privacy, and your freedom will be the determining factors that drive you to create your ideal lifestyle. For each dimension of your lifestyle, decide what actions you can start taking today to make each component a ten! What could possibly stand in the way of you being a ten? You can become the captain of your own destiny. It is totally up to you.

Constructing your optimal lifestyle starts with envisioning what is ideal for you at home, work, and play. Your imagination and your mind power are the origins of your dream. Put yourself to the task, and warm up to your dream-come-true lifestyle. Ponder these following questions in a quiet, meditative setting. Discover for yourself what you really feel most strongly about. Gain some clarity on what it might be worth to you to be healthy, happy, and free (free to spend your time as you see fit).

- Were you to inherit a few million dollars, who would you be, how would you live, and how would this change your life?
- What are the highest principles in your life?
- What are you looking for in a soul mate?
- What do you want to say with your life?
- What do you want to accomplish with your life?
- What kind of qualities do you want to be known for?
- What price are you willing to pay for good health and daily happiness?
- What price are you willing to pay to be successful and rich?
- What brings you the greatest happiness?
- What are you ready to commit to in this lifetime?
- What kind of work do you find most satisfying?

Keep Track of How You Spend Your Time

With a sharper sense of self-awareness, you can determine how you choose to budget your time. No matter how you do it, there are only twenty-four hours, 1,440 minutes, 86,400 seconds in a day. The focus is on how to make the most efficient use of your time and energy. For the next few days, keep a log of your daily activities listed below. Remember to observe and record how you feel inside while you spend your time on each activity.

Activity	Amount of Time	Inner Lifestyle (happy, relaxed, rushed, stressed)
intrapersonal growth		
(self-nourishment, time with nature)		
interpersonal relationships		
family relationships		
social relationships		
career or work		
eating		
sleeping		
household chores		
personal grooming		
recreational sports		
telephone and personal business		

Activity	Amount of Time	Inner Lifestyle
hobbies		
passive activities (TV, radio, spectator sports, reading)		
studying and writing		
entertainment		
having fun/kicking back		

Putting Your Priorities in Order

A healthy lifestyle is a meaningful and balanced lifestyle. This means that you are doing what you truly love to do within the context of a responsible adult behavior. There is a science to creating a balanced lifestyle. Its foundation relies upon your ability to recognize the priorities in your life. *When the way you spend your time fully supports making time for what you value the most,* then it can be said that your lifestyle is in harmony with your priorities. Your priorities are the driving forces that mold your lifestyle into shape. Your priorities are heavily influenced by your belief systems and your personal philosophy on the meaning of your life. It is your privilege and it is to your advantage to get your priorities in order. When you are in harmony with yourself and your priorities, this is High Performance Living.

What means more to you than anything else?

What are your beliefs about the importance of
        love?   children?

        health?   work?

        marriage?   sex?

What is your personal philosophy of life (what makes you tick?)

What are the main priorities in your life? List them from highest
to lowest.
        1)_____
        2)_____
        3)_____
        4)_____
        5)_____
        6)_____
Are you spending your time in proportion with your highest
priorities? Or, like most individuals, do you spend too much
time on lower priorities (financial security, power, business,
money, possessions) at the expense of not having enough time
with higher priority issues (wellness, happiness, spirituality,
nourishing loved ones, family)? The key is to balance your
highest priorities to create High Performance Living at intrapersonal, interpersonal, and career related levels.

Establish Your Goals

Recognizing your priorities is the most direct path to designing a balanced lifestyle. Invariably, your soul-searching will get you in touch with your most personal goals. Your goals give you priorities, aim, and direction. The question is, are your goals in sync with your priorities?

Organize your goals into the following categories. Write down your goals, and be very specific. Are these lifetime objectives being supported by your present lifestyle?

1) Intrapersonal—how would you like to see yourself in the future?

2) Interpersonal/Family Relationships

3) Professional/Career or Work Goals

4) Leisure Time/Recreational Goals

5) Financial Goals

6) Travel, Adventure, and Educational Goals

7) Artistic Goals

Plan Out Your Three-Month Goals

To move from the ideal to the practical, the imagined to the realistic, identify your seasonal goals. At each seasonal change, review your goals for the coming season. Keep yourself updated every three months. Use the same categories listed for your lifetime goals.

Managing Time to Meet Your Goals

The prioritization of your goals determines how you make the absolute best use of your time and resources. Classify the most important goal as priority #1, the next most important as priority #2, and so on down the line. If you were told that you only had six months to live, would that change your goals, priorities, and lifestyle?

Turn your focus back to your daily schedule. Creating the most idealized lifestyle calls for budgeting time each day for the high-priority events in your life.

Early Morning Before 8 A.M.	Morning 8–11:30 A.M.
Mid-day 11:30–1:30	Early Afternoon 1:30–4 P.M.

Late Afternoon 4–6 P.M.	Early Evening 6–8 P.M.
Late Evening 8–11 P.M.	Late-Late 11:30–on

Usually, there are sixteen hours a day to work with when scheduling your daily activities. Eight hours typically are used for sleep and personal hygiene. Block out a set of time for:

- Yourself
- Your Loved Ones
- Playtime
- Your Most Important Projects
- Making a Living

The bottom line is:

- Schedule at least one hour a day for personal growth.
- Leave at least one hour a day for your primary love relationship.
- Allow one hour a day for quality time with your family and/or children. For those without close family, put in time for a dear friend.
- Designate one hour for outdoor physical or recreational time (weather permitting).

The above will take at least four hours a day: this leaves you twelve hours for the rest of your day. Schedule your highest priorities during peak times. What time of the day are you most productive? Do routine chores during non-key times. Your work, basic chores, time for personal hygiene, relaxation time, time for laying back, or time for whatever has to get done will fill in the rest. Balancing your day between your needs and your necessities will bear the fruits of a healthy lifestyle.

Organizing the Necessities of Life

While you are at it, here are some tips on organizing the necessities of life.

1) Clothing—get rid of uncomfortable clothes. Repair clothes. Make sure you have clothing for working out, bathing suit and cap, etc.

   Shoes—be kind to your feet. If the shoe does not fit, do not wear it.

   Colors—take heed to everything about you that gives the message of who you are. Wear colors that make you feel good.

2) Car—clean it completely; make needed repairs. What does your car say about you?

3) Your home—is it orderly, neat? What do you like to have around you—flowers, books, food, art?

4) Shopping—find out when deliveries are made at the store of your choice so that you do not have to keep going back. Plan your shopping time during non-peak hours. Do not shop when you are hungry; you are more likely to make expensive, convenience food decisions.

5) Banking—set your finances in order. Balance your checkbook. Determine how to make your banking more efficient (bank by phone, automated teller machine). Keep your bank balance updated. Set aside time once a month to pay all bills.

6) Telephone—Use the time you talk on the phone for tasks such as cleaning your fingernails, stretching, balancing exercises.

7) Household—Stock up on toilet paper, soap, sponges, cleaning items, everyday household necessities. When you see a sale, stock up on the item to save time and money.

8) Personal Files—Go through your files, and throw away unnecessary items. If you do not have a filing system, create one.

9) Professional Files—Update professional and business files.

10) Tool Kit—Take inventory of your tool kit to include a screwdriver, nails, hammer, flashlight, extension cord, etc. Make an agreement to keep tools in their place.

11) Create a space for personal office supplies, tape, pencils and pens, stapler, paper, envelopes, and stamps.

12) Put a pad and plenty of pens by the telephone.

13) Update your address book.

14) Keep a list of your most frequently called numbers handy by the telephone. Update it periodically.

15) Lighten up your environment. Go through your house totally, and give away what does not work or what you do not need. Have a garage sale. Recycle, and make your house environmentally sound.

16) Have a place to keep keys and wallet or purse so you do not waste time looking for them.

17) Take pride in whatever you do.

18) Use waiting time (on phone or in line) as a gift of time to relax, and learn how to be patient.

19) Keep a list handy of things you need to accomplish for the week, for the day. Prioritize your list.
20) Review your schedule the night before so it will be organized when you wake-up. This way, you do not have to think about it during self-nurturing time.
21) Block out three-hour time frames for major projects.
22) Whistle, sing, and enjoy yourself while you work.

Direct Decision Making

Finally, have a system for making important decisions. A direct decision calls for sound judgment based on the benefit/risk ratio.

Making Appropriate Decisions for the Future

1) Define the nature of the conflict that you need to resolve.
2) List possible choices (including brainstorming to seek fresh approaches).
3) Also, list pros and cons of each choice.
4) Weigh all factors, and determine which choice has the most benefits and the least risks. Circle your best choice.
5) Go into a deep meditation to clear your mind. Spend time in a relaxed natural quiet setting. Let your intuition guide you to choose the best solution.
6) Act on that solution. Follow through, be persistent and focused.

Example:
Define your conflict: I don't know which job to choose.

Choice 1: Downtown Firm

Benefits	Risks
a) better pay	a) less personal time for me
b) good location	b) unknown company
c) numerous opportunities	c) no medical benefits

Define your conflict:

Choice 1

Benefits	Risks
a)	a)
b)	b)
c)	c)

Define your conflict:

Choice 2

Benefits	Risks
a)	a)
b)	b)
c)	c)

Always remember that if you get stuck, keep positive, fine tune, and go back through the benefit/risk ratio decision making process until you feel comfortable with your choice.

Dr. Barnet's Formula for Creating a Balanced Lifestyle

You are responsible for creating a self-sufficient, self-reliant life-style. First:

- Elevate your consciousness through guided introspection.
- Determine the highest priorities in your life.
- Make a full commitment to your priorities.
- Take the responsibility for realizing your priorities.
- Size up your present lifestyle.
- Outline your ideal lifestyle.
- Set up your lifetime goals. Be specific.
- Outline your goals for the next three months. Be specific.
- Harmonize your priorities with your goals into a daily schedule.
- Overcome any obstacles.
- Set up a daily plan of action.
- Bring the idealized future into the present by the total satisfaction of wholly living in the moment.

Never lose sight of the fact that it is totally up to you to create a self-sufficient, self-reliant lifestyle. Keep it simple, keep it light, stay balanced, and be abundant. Be assured that with the right attitude, you can have fun while taking full responsibility for realizing your highest priorities. You can overcome any obstacles and have a fulfilled, relaxed, productive, balanced lifestyle. This is the challenge every human being faces. To be realized, to be ful-filled, to be happy, to be vital, to die well with a smile on your face, to love life and appreciate being alive. This is the quest. Stick to your principles and recruit dynamic willpower. I believe the Ten Rules of High Performance Living will give you the tools to invite this commitment into every moment of your life.

Index

Italicized entries indicate pages with quizzes; bold entries indicate pages with question-and-answer worksheets.

110. *See also* cleansing, nutritional; maintenance diet

nutritional cleansing. *See* cleansing, nutritional

nutritional discretionary quotient, 116–24, **120**

nutritional supplements: cleansing diet, 92; maintenance diet, 146

O

obligations, unnecessary, **18–19**

overeating, 152

P

passive relaxation, 35

peace of mind, 188–89, **189**

perseverance, emotional, 79–80

personal organization, 220–22

physical fitness: aerobic conditioning, 157–60; assessing, *153–56*; benefits of, 151–53; building stamina, 160; cardiovascular fitness, 152; cycling program, 164–66; definition of, 151; exercises, 160–61; jogging program, 158–60; lifestyle changes, **156**; and metabolism,

151–52; and overeating, 152; preparation, 161, **161**; spinal flexibility, 160; swimming program, 161–63; target heart rate, 157; walking program, 166–67

physical fitness quiz, *153–56*

phytonutrients, 112

poisons, nutritional, 85–86

positive thinking, 36

power consciousness, 181

prayer, 11. *See also* soul, healing the

priorities, 215–16, **215–16**

priorities and needs: balancing, 14–15, **15**; defining, 1–4

protein, complete: breakfast menu combinations, 132; dinner menu combinations, 135–37; luncheon menu combinations, 133–35; in the maintenance diet, 131–32; typical daily menus, 138–39

purpose in life: effects of losing, 192–94; finding, **197–98**, 197–202, **200**, *201–2*, 204–5, **205**; importance of finding, 191–92, 194–96; multiple purposes, 196; personal responsibility, 196; pursuing passions, 200–202, *201–2*; sexuality issues, 202–4

target heart rate, 157
target organs, 26–27
tests. *See* quizzes
time allocation, 214–15,
  214–15
time management, **218–19**,
  218–20
Tofu Chop Suey, 147–48

V

values, identifying, 1–4
Vegetable Broth, Dr. Meltzer's
  Potassium-Rich, 105
Vegetable Casserole, 149

victimization, feelings of,
  54–55

W

walking program, 166–67
wellness, 23
white flour, 126
willpower, 60–61, **61**, 189

Y

yoga, 160, 178

3773

About the Author

 Barnet Meltzer, M.D., has been a Board Certified physician and surgeon for twenty-five years. Dr. Meltzer graduated Phi Beta Kappa from the University of Pennsylvania School of Medicine and did his internship at UCLA. He then served two years as a resident surgeon at the University of California Medical Center in San Diego. He owns the distinction of being the first medical doctor to enter the clinical practice of Preventive Medicine and Alternative Medicine in southern California. He retains a thriving practice in Del Mar, California. He is a pioneer and well-known authority in the field of Clinical Nutrition and Wellness-related Preventive Medicine, and is a former professor, health advisor to Olympic athletes, and radio talk show host. He has an international reputation, having brought his teachings to South America, Mexico, Central America, and the South Pacific.